TO SFBC —

Enjoy the journey.

T. W. Lawrence

The Trail Ends in Texas

The Trail Ends in Texas

The Complete "Dusty and the Cowboy" Trilogy

by

T. W. Lawrence

Dedication

This anthology is dedicated to all those who've been lost in this life, taking the wrong trail – whether they knew better or not.

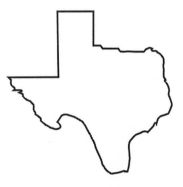

Acknowledgments

If I've learned nothing else in these last few months, it's that writing a book is not something done alone.

I would like to express my heartfelt appreciation for those who helped make me look so good on paper:

My editor: **Fran Lawrence**

My cover artist: **Vanessa Lowry**

My print production manager: **Jessica Parker**

My audio producer: **Sandy Weaver**

My question writer: **Bryan Tyson**

My audiobook narrator: **Moby (Moby in the Morning)**

Special thanks to **Michael Belk** for his great photo used on the front cover. To see more of his work and the path he is now taking, please visit:

www.journeyswiththemessaih.com.

Thank you all,
T.W. Lawrence

Table of Contents

Foreword

I have eagerly awaited the publication of *Coming Home*, the final book in the *Dusty and the Cowboy* trilogy. I have successfully used the first two books, *Lord Show Me the Way* and *Rendezvous*, in our outreach ministry with Cowboys For Christ. *Lord Show Me the Way* is a great tool to use for the person that has not yet had an experience with Christ. The stories in book two, *Rendezvous*, show how Cowboy, the main character, came to know Christ for himself. *Coming Home* will help all of us to reflect on our Christian journey after meeting Christ, whether that be for a day or for decades.

I met the author, T.W. Lawrence, at a cowboy gathering, while I was manning a tent for Cowboys for Christ. This was about the time he released the first book in his trilogy. It became clear that we shared the same passion to reach the lost for Jesus Christ and to encourage people in their Christian walk. Being a cowboy at heart, Cowboys for Christ has given me that opportunity by becoming a Cowboy Chaplain. T.W. shared with me that his goal was not to sell books, but to use the *Dusty and the Cowboy* trilogy for the building and strengthening of the Kingdom of God.

T.W.'s idea to reach the lost, as well as the believer, by using short books of cowboy Christian Historical Fiction, written in easy-to-read prose, clearly works. Each book is organized in chapters, each of which tells a story that compliments the theme of the book. The study questions at the end of each chapter are very useful for individual or group study. I know of several people using these books in Sunday school and for men's Bible study. T.W.'s books are easy to pick up and put down, and they will appeal to those who would not normally read a novel.

T.W., being a native Texan and the son of a veterinarian, uses his background and experiences to make these stories come alive. His characters are believable, and his descriptions vivid, and his facts accurate. T.W.'s research is apparent, and his personal faith and walk with Christ come through in his writing.

Dusty and the Cowboy conveys the message of salvation and living the Christian life without being preachy. I have yet to share

one of these books without a request for the next in the series. I am confident you as the reader will not be disappointed. The saying that no hour spent in the saddle is an hour wasted could also be applied to these books. Just sit back and enjoy a good read.
God Bless!

Bob Perkerson

Cowboy Chaplain
Cowboys for Christ

Cattle Trails

PART 1

Lord, Show Me The Way

Dusty

He slowly dismounted from the horse, and stood in the dust examining the trail. He'd been to Cowtown once or twice in his adult life, but it had been awhile. From this point, just across the river there were two well-traveled ways to get there. There was also a lesser path, more dangerous in the steeps and falls, but the scenery was said to be spectacular.

It should have been an obvious choice, but his mind was full of other thoughts, and now and then his heart grew heavy. As a cowpoke, he was more than fair. He could ride and rope with the best of them. He was a natural at handling the livestock, and he could toss a steer without much trouble.

Dusty, his horse of many years, was getting older now. Gently, he rubbed its nose and offered up a chunk of salt, which was the horse's favorite. Thinking still about the changes to the cowboy way, he knew *that* life had run its course. It was time to move on to what he would do next.

"Dear Lord, you have always guided my footsteps, whether I asked for help or not. Well, sir, now I'm askin' for that help. Me and Dusty got a ways to go. But sure as I'm standin' here, I'm in a ponder as to the best way to git there. Preacher man always says You got the way for us. Not that it's the easiest way or even the way we'd take, given our own choosin'. But it's the way we should be goin'."

He looked down at the broad weathered hat in his hands. "Lord, show me that way."

With these thoughts on his mind, he mounted Dusty. Spurring the big horse, he gave it free reign. A notion came to let Dusty pick the path. After all, we're all God's creatures. Maybe Dusty knew the answers that today he did not.

From his vest pocket, the cowboy pulled a sheet of tattered paper, folded and creased with wear. Neat ink lettering penned long ago, was barely legible now from calloused fingers touching it so many times. "Preacher man said these words might help," he told Dusty. "It's from Revelation. 'For the Lamb at the center of the throne will be their shepherd; he will lead them to springs of living water.'"

In response, Dusty nickered once over his shoulder. Then he bobbed his head, and began to trot down the trail in long, easy strides.

Their journey had begun.

Dusty
Study Questions

1. Cowboy faced a big decision: which fork in the trail to take. What is a major decision you have had to make in life? How did you decide what was the best decision? How did your decision work out?

2. Cowboy prayed and asked God to show him the way, then allowed Dusty to choose the trail. Do you think God directed Dusty to the right trail? Why or why not?

3. The Bible verse Cowboy read talks about the Lamb being the shepherd for his people. What does a shepherd have to do for the sheep? How does God do those things for us?

Biscuits

"Hello in the camp!" the cowboy yelled. He stood up in his stirrups, one hand grasping the saddle's horn, the other holding Dusty's reins ever so lightly. The lone figure crouching near the fire, some thirty yards distant, turned a grizzled face in Cowboy's direction. A worn poke-sack lay on the ground beside him. From it the old man drew out a rusted Navy Colt pistol, the kind that sported the clumsy cap and ball ammunition.

"Who are you then?" he called back in a reedy voice. "And, how many?" The heavy weapon swayed back and forth held by an unsteady hand.

Cowboy urged the big buckskin horse forward out of the darkness. "Just me and Dusty," he said. "Saw your fire from that rise a ways back. Thought I'd chance some hot grub and a little conversation." Keeping both hands in plain view of the stranger, the cowboy dismounted with unhurried movements. "Trail gets lonely and even hardtack tastes some sourish ten days in a row."

The old-timer wiped filmy eyes with the back of a tattered sleeve, squinting to see the cowboy, now visible in the fire's glow. Taking his time judging this unexpected wrangler's intent, he finally offered, "Food's hard to come by in these parts, 'less you're partial to cactus flesh. Plenty of that hereabouts. But if'n you've beans and such, I got biscuit makin's. We kin trade. Coffee's weak, but it's hot."

The cowboy tied the horse's leathers to a mesquite bough. From the saddlebag on Dusty's rump he took the bag of dried frijoles, a cut of deer jerky, and the dented metal cup he used for coffee.

Cowboy relaxed when his elderly host dispatched the huge revolver back to its hidey place in the poke. He judged from the aged appearance that the gun's powder likely might never spark, leaving it useless against beasts, marauders, or savages. He wondered why the man even bothered to tote it around at all.

Using a small shovel, the old-timer raked live coals to a pile in front of the homemade Dutch oven. After which he inspected the miner's pan used for making biscuits, and found it somewhat in a neglected state. The man grabbed up a handful of sand and rubbed the pan's bottom with unaccustomed vigor until the layer of grit scrubbed off. All the time the man kneaded dough, stirred beans, fried and baked, a lively whistled tune or some distracted humming accompanied his every move.

When the meal drew down to the last uneaten biscuit, Cowboy allowed as how cooking was always better when someone else had done it. The old man had been right about the coffee -- hot and not much else. It carried that hardpan taste of caliche, where those minerals had seeped into the waterholes thereabouts. But the cowboy did not dwell on that. Instead, he listened as the other spun yarns of a prospector always one day's sift away from striking the money ores.

Cowboy tossed his coffee dregs and snatched the last biscuit from the pan. "You don't sound like you're from around here," he said. "Where you call home?"

"Nowhere's in particular," the old man replied.

"You got people back wherever that is?" Cowboy asked innocent enough, but the man stared back wild-eyed. Cowboy had seen that look before; a crippled bobcat, back broken by a deadfall trap. Its eyes conveyed a staggering fear coupled with growing resignation. But he still dared a determination not to die. It had been a haunting moment. The man stared at the fire without a word. Crackle of dry mesquite burning made the only sound for several minutes.

"Was a gal," he began without looking up. "Pretty thing. We courted and sparked more'n a year 'fore I come out West to make my riches. Promised her I'd come back a wealthy man to marry her." From his appearance that had yet to happen. The man kept his gaze to the ground.

"Where is she now?" Cowboy asked.

"Can't say as I know for sure," the old man answered with shaky intonation. "Still there, I reckon."

Cowboy rubbed the bottom of his jaw with bare knuckles of his free hand. He shook his head in thought. "You ever get back there on occasion?"

Started to once or twice," the man said. "Third time I got as far as the railhead other side of them mountains yonder." He pointed off in the darkness. "Couldn't make myself get on that train. Sent her a telegram instead. Then I got knee-walking drunk." He poked dying embers with a stick, stirring them into random rows. "Next morning I woke up face down in wet clay behind some privy. Western Union man had stuffed an envelope in my pocket. The lady had wrote me back."

The old-timer's thin shoulders began to heave and fall in rapid order. A stifled moan, painful to Cowboy's ears, clung in the man's throat for what seemed like an eternity. His bushy brows touched wet cheeks as he kept eyes screwed shut. When the prospector collected himself a bit, he said, "I had enough talk for one night. Set your soogans where you will." Then he tromped to a spot near his pile of possessions, threw a blanket on the sand, and wrapped himself in it.

The old man spoke nothing further, so Cowboy stood to stretch. He fetched the bedroll from his saddle, unrolling it on a suitable piece of ground. He made sure Dusty was set for the night, settled himself into a comfortable pose for slumber, and went immediately to sleep.

* * *

Dawn was no more than the first grey streaks against the clouds on the far horizon. Cowboy had watered and saddled Dusty, and stowed all his gear back in the saddlebags. He could tell from Dusty's stirring that the big horse wanted to be on the move already. The old man still lay under the blanket, floppy hat covering most of the whiskered face. Cowboy's Ma and Pa had raised all their sons to be hard-working but polite. This meant that he could not leave without thanking the man for his hospitality, and especially the biscuits. That included the one Cowboy now carried in his coat pocket to eat later on.

"*Viejo*," he called out gently to the old-timer, not wanting to spook the man out here in this big stretch of lonely sand hills. The Spanish term seemed appropriate since it meant venerated elder. The prospector did not dignify Cowboy with a response, in either language, not so much as even a twitch. When the man remained unmoved at the second mild beckoning, Cowboy knelt beside the quiet figure to shake him with a light grip on his bony shoulder. It took no more than a second to realize the old man was dead.

The cowboy stood, removing the hat from his head. "I swear, Dusty, if that don't beat all. It's like he was just waiting for someone to come along so he wouldn't have to die alone. And that someone is us."

Cowboy studied the lifeless form at his feet, but despite his wish for a miraculous revival it didn't happen. He gazed at the few scattered possessions belonging to the man: shovel, pick, daypack, Dutch oven, and the bulging poke-sack. It occurred to him that in keeping with custom in these parts Cowboy had not asked the man's name - even when he had spoken his own and gotten nothing in return. If there were to be a clue as to any next-of-kin it would be found in the poke.

Emptying the sack's contents on the ground, he found only three items: the Colt, a leather-bound book, and a small pouch. Cowboy selected the book first. He was surprised to find that it was a Bible. "I didn't figure you for a man of Scripture," he said looking over `his shoulder. "Not my place to judge, but I'd calculate it was something else you struggled with."

Then Cowboy picked up the pouch. In it he found a locket of heavy gold roughly the size and heft of a pocket watch. Its fine chain held the locket's hasp at one end and the other attached to a small gentleman's folding knife decorated with hammered gold. Cowboy thumbed the locket open. It swung easily on hinges often used. Engraved on one side's smooth interior, in an elaborate Gothic script, were the words: "Two Hearts Entwined – One Love Forever." Beneath that, the name: "Adeline". The matching side held a faded Daguerreotype image of a young woman. Her beauty in the photo had not diminished over time. Cowboy was drawn at once to the liveliness sparkling in her eyes. "So you're the one," he said to the face in the locket.

That's when he saw the slip of paper still hiding in the pouch. It bore the markings of a telegraph form. The top corner had been torn off long ago, and with that went the receiver's name. The penciled words were few: "I don't need the gold. I need the man. Come back to me." It was signed: "Addy." Cowboy could feel the tightness beginning at his throat, hard as a peach pit. He also felt the warmth rising at the back of his neck. It continued to burn halfway up his scalp. "Are you a complete ignorant?" Cowboy said loud enough to startle Dusty. "She implored you back to her, but you couldn't even muster the courage to put your fears aside." His fury roiled at the thought of their missed reconciliation. But anger aside, Cowboy discovered no means among the prospector's things to inform anyone of the old-timer's passing.

It took more than two hours of spading in the hard ground beneath the sand to dig out a sufficient grave. The old man was placed there, with his hat, brogans, and other trappings; arms crossed at the chest. Cowboy slid the locket beneath one hand and the paper beneath the other. The bible he nestled against the belly, the Colt at the hip. Finally, he draped the blanket atop the length of the body.

"I ain't no preacher man but I'll say these words: 'I pray you meet your Adeline again on the Streets of Glory in a way you never could here on this earthly plane. Amen." Spade by spade, Cowboy filled the grave. He covered that with stones from nearby.

As he untied Dusty, he said to the buckskin, "I promise you this. I'll never die a crazy old coot out in the desert, too proud to go back to them that love me." Dusty turned his head so that one dark eye was level with Cowboy's. "What are you, my conscience now?" the cowboy asked his horse. "There's no doubt I was prideful as a young'un. Ma, God rest her soul, would ask what I was doing about that. I'd tell her, 'God's working on my humility.' She'd just give me that smile that made you feel loved down to the very quick, and say, "No, God's working on your lack of humility. Better keep after it.'"

He grinned. For a moment Cowboy stood motionless as he fought back tears brimming at the corner of his eye. Seconds passed. Then he stepped a boot into the stirrup and swung a leg over Dusty, seating himself squarely in the saddle. Cowboy tugged the reins hard left, turning the horse around to the trail they'd come down just the night before. He tapped the buckskin's flank with the quirt, first to a trot then to a canter. Cowboy eased a hand into the coat pocket as he did so. He felt the irregular roundness of the biscuit, still smooth to the touch. Its being there reminded him that he still had miles to go before sundown. And an old man's dying words to ponder.

From the coat's other pocket Cowboy tugged loose the small hardback given him when he'd first set out from home, a traveler's Bible. He pressed it open with the heel of his palm and balancing it on his thigh. Long fingers flicked through pages until he arrived at the chosen verse: Joshua, Chapter 1.

Cowboy had found a ribbon, probably Addy's, at this very spot in the old man's Scriptures. Selected words in the prospector's bible, in verses 8 and 9, had been marked by some dull underscore. He read them out now to Dusty, in rhythm to the hoof beats pounding on the trail: "For then thou shalt make thy way prosperous, and then thou shalt have good success... Be strong and of good courage; be not afraid, neither be thou dismayed."

The cowboy mulled those words over once. Then twice. In due time, he shared his thoughts, "A man's mind can dwell on part of a thing, and set the rest aside. That man can stumble when the whole of that lesson is missed." In farewell to the old-timer buried back beneath the rocks he said, "What you done, or what you ain't – that's between you and God Almighty. I got chore enough just minding after my own fretful soul. Rest in peace, *viejo.*"

Under the blue expanse of a now cloudless sky, Cowboy and Dusty loped the trail together at an easy pace.

Their journey had begun.

Biscuits
Study Questions

1. The old man didn't want to go back to his true love until he had enough money to give. The telegram showed she wasn't interested in the money—she wanted him. How is the woman the old man loved like Jesus wanting us to come home to a relationship with him? Do we need to clean ourselves up or become good before we go home to him? Why or why not?

2. Cowboy says that God keeps working on his humility. Why would God want us to have humility? How does a humble heart allow us to have a better relationship with God and others?

3. Cowboy read the verses from Joshua about God leading us and having courage. Why does the fact that God leads us give us courage to face difficult situations? How can you think differently about challenges you face because you know God is leading?

Jumping Dog

Every wrangler worth his four bits a day knows a horse hears sound more keenly than any man. In a minute more, Cowboy heard it, too. Low and guttural.

The growling floated up on gusts blowing out of the arroyos stretched out below. These winds blew dry warmth against the wrangler's already leathered features. He studied the sound a moment, straining to hear all its varied tones. His imagination told him that if he closed his eyes and drew breath across his tongue, he could single out this unseen creature by its smell alone.

Cowboy smiled a knowing smile. That was but another boyhood fantasy he carried along the trail with him like some unneeded catstick or jinglebob.

Whatever might be down the way, now hidden by the crest of the upcoming hilltop, it stopped Dusty in his tracks and had the big horse mighty skittish.

Cowboy pressed back against the cantle, leaning down to grab the Winchester 73. With a big hand through the loop, he slid the rifle out of the scabbard. Cowboy laid its octagonal barrel across his lap while stirring Dusty into a walk with the heel of his boot. Holding both reins in one hand as they crested the ridge, Cowboy surveyed the scene below intent on spying the source of this commotion. What he saw down in the undersized valley did nothing more than puzzle him.

Near the narrow depression that formed the western entrance, a grey *lupito* sat motionless on its haunches in a half-crouch. The mere scent of this animal on the breeze was enough to disquiet his trusted horse. By its markings, Cowboy reckoned this to be the

15

Mexican Wolf, *el lobo mexicano* in the native tongue. The lone creature had the broad head, thick neck, and long ears of the breed. Its tan body carried dark streaks across the back and on the head, cleanly offset by a white muzzle and throat. It was the desert's fiercest carnivore. At intervals, the wolf lifted its nose to sniff out some quarry nearby. Cowboy swung his vision eastward to see what that might be.

At the valley's center a brockle-faced Hereford huddled near her calf. The baby lurched repeatedly. It stood in the midst of a metamorphic rock outcropping bordered closely by thick cholla. That cactus stood nearly tall as a man. The calf yanked forward over and again, but could not progress from the spot. Its hind left hoof seemed caught in the rock somehow. Mama's head down in defiance, she faced the oncoming predator with herself placed between it and her offspring. But the main curiosity to Cowboy was a solitary rider halted atop a small knoll further to the east, astride a beautiful bangtail mustang. Both were partially hidden behind a sizeable century plant's full rosette. The young puncher watched this life-and-death drama unfolding before him as though hypnotized.

In an instant, the wolf broke from his crouch, loping fast toward the outcropping and the Herefords. Before it could cover more than twenty yards, Cowboy raised the weapon to his shoulder and fired. The bullet careened off a flat rock near el lobo's front feet. The second landed beneath the body, 'tween front and hind legs. That kicked up sand, stinging the belly and causing the wolf to flinch. Rather than bolting all at once, the predator merely turned its big head toward the sound of the rifle's report to assess his current circumstance. Apparently choosing to live to hunt another day, he whirled on furry heels and trotted in no particular hurry out of the valley.

The young rider turned to the sound as well, but aside from staring gave no acknowledgement to Cowboy's presence or what he'd just done. Instead, he fanned the pony with his hat and began to pick his way through the debris field to get to the Herefords in more or less a straight line.

Cowboy urged Dusty into a trot. Together they descended the hilltop, and turned in to the mouth of the valley. Reining the buckskin in as he approached the rider and the beeves, Cowboy recognized the brand burned into the mama's hide to be the same one on the pony's hip -- the unmistakable and well-known Half-Diamond-Bar.

With the wolf gone now, the young puncher had come to claim the ranch's stock. Not that he would have, had the lobo been able to finish the hunt. "I'd tell you much obliged for helping out, pardner," Cowboy said in a churlish tenor. "'Cept I seen but *nada* from you so far." He glared across at the other rider, angry at the man's laziness or downright ineptitude when it came to riding for the brand. He expected a mealy-mouth reply. Instead, what Cowboy saw staring back at him caused a smile to curl at the corners of his mouth. A lad of no more than sixteen years sat wordless on the spirited pinto *mestengo*. The boy was outfitted without question completely in hand-me-downs, and at that, all with articles befitting a much larger man.

"I see you're chuckin' the Rio," Cowboy said with a laugh this time. "And doing it right dandy, too."

"What's that mean, mister?" the young rider said in a voice not yet settled into manhood.

"In these parts, it's how we dub outsiders dressin' theirselves to look like Texans who been reared all their lives in Rio Grande cattle country. But trying too hard and getting it wrong mostly." The boy's hat spread wide as a sombrero, but with the brim turned down both front and back at a jack-deuce angle. Its crown stood tall, deep dimples creased at all four compass points in what the locals called the Montana Peak. The shirt bore no collar, its unbuttoned long-sleeves pushed back on slender forearms, held there by gaudy red garters. A bandana the size of a ship's sail encircled his neck, hiding most of the thin chest. No chaps covered his baggy pants. They were poked into scuffed boots with worn Mexican heels and blunted oversized spurs. Cowboy judged the lad must be wearing layers of stockings or some other thick stuffings just to keep those boots from sliding off his feet. But the youngster's eyes stayed fixed on Cowboy's -- guarded, never wavering.

"What do they call you?" Cowboy asked. "And where you hail from? The Southern states, I expect."

"My given name is Toby Guinn," the boy answered. "But all the ranch hands call me Pup, on account of I'm such a greenhorn." His face didn't change as he spoke. It maintained a placid wariness that masked his private thoughts. "I come out of the Kinchafoonee community down along the Flint River, back in Georgia."

"Well if you don't mind my asking, Pup," Cowboy ventured. "Them's cattle from your herd. How come you made no move to unsettle the wolf? Or rescue the calf from its confines? Ain't that your job?

"Truth be told, sir, they don't actually let me handle the livestock," Pup said. "I'm just the chooch in the outfit. This morning I was to ride fence and make repair. Found barbed-wire down and saw strays over in that coulee." He tossed a head over his shoulder, indicating where he had come from. "Then I heard all this bawling. Came over to see what all the hullabaloo was about, just before you fired those shots." For the first time he broke Cowboy's gaze. He stared somewhere around Dusty's nose. "Didn't figure to tangle with no wolf."

"First one you come upon?" Cowboy asked with a certain softness.

"Yes, sir. Never saw anything like that before. A wolf, I mean." Pup raised his head once more. "Like you read about in all Mr. Grimm's Tales. Lots bigger than a coyote, of which I've seen plenty back home. And I swear there was death in those eyes of his."

Cowboy studied the boy for a moment. "No matter. We got the calf to pull free. It might be injured by now." He eyed the mama cow now guarding its baby against the two new interlopers with the same determination as before. "You're a mite smaller than me," Cowboy went on. "Why don't you sidle twixt the cholla and that critter. Shouldn't catch too many thorns. Yank the leg free while I keep the mama at bay. Your chance to be a real stock handler for once."

Pup said nothing. He just gritted his teeth, shaking his head back-and-forth in a most emphatic negative, underneath that big hat. "Can't," he said at last. "Just can't. A cactus that can jump like that could be the death of me." Pup clenched his jaw so hard that silent tears began to streak down his cheeks. Wetness might have marked his frustration, but it sprang from the deep shame of his unconquerable fear.

Cowboy clearly did not understand the young rider's disconcertment, but knew he must attend to the still struggling calf before any real harm befell it. Dismounting Dusty, he untied his coat and rain slicker from the back of the saddle. Cowboy donned them both, buttoning each and turning up the slicker's collar before tying his bandana around it tight. At the last, he pulled his hat full down, making certain it covered the back of his neck. With care, hunching and crawling on all fours, Cowboy made his way to the calf. He could feel cactus needles scratching the oilcloth that covered his shoulders. The closer he got, the more agitated the young Hereford became. It bawled even louder as the man's gloved hand first touched it. Cowboy ran his fingers along the hip and down the leg, stopping just above the hock.

He craned to look into the dark crevice holding the hoof. Cowboy could just make out that a loose stone, probably freed up by the calf's erratic stepping, had trapped the hoof against a notch that formed the better part of the hole. Free it, and free the hoof he figured. But to do that meant Cowboy would have to wedge himself behind the calf and move up against the thickest limbs of the cholla patch. The whelp's continuous gyrations made that job even the more chancy, but Cowboy felt he had no other choice.

In place at last, the tall man heaved a shoulder into the animal's rump to create some slack on the hoof and the stone. Using a great effort, and three tries, Cowboy finally pried the rock from its confinement. With the hoof now loose at last and the animal's need for survival at its peak, the calf rewarded Cowboy with what instinct demanded it must do. It kicked him hard in the chest with the freed limb, catching Cowboy off guard and out-of-balance. He tripped over his own boots and fell backwards as though thrown from a horse. As the cow and baby scampered away, Cowboy cussed the calf, cussed himself, and cussed the Jumping Dog Cholla in whose arms with the thousand needles he now rested.

Surprised that he could feel no pain except the sharp soreness at his breast, Cowboy considered how to get off his back and onto his feet without sticking himself needlessly. He knew that rolling one way or the other, or even shifting his weight to lift himself by the palms of his hand would surely puncture his protective clothing. The answer came as the knotted end of a lariat landed on his belly. Cowboy looked up to see that Pup had the other end tied around his saddle horn.

"Not a bad toss for a Arbuckle tenderfoot," Cowboy said with a cautious smile. "Now ease him back real slow." The pinto responded to Pup's gentle command, taking slack out of the rope with each deliberate step. Soon Cowboy stood upright on the outcropping. The brim of his hat and the entire back of his slicker were festooned with a complete host of cactus barbs, big and small, too numerous to count. It looked like Aunt Nellie's pincushion. But as Cowboy moved his arms back to his side, he felt the sting of cactus stickers imbedded in his skin rubbing against the cuff of the coat. "DANG it. That smarts!"

Under Pup's watchful stare, Cowboy managed to strip off the outerwear without inflicting further pain. His left wrist held two dozen smaller barbs, and twice that number of the tiny needles. From his vest he took out the pocket knife. Using it and a thumb, Cowboy managed to pull out the bigger stickers. Each extraction caused him to wince and draw blood.

"I judge the scrape with that cholla might have turned out more poorly," Cowboy said. "But this old slicker took the most of it." He held the oilcloth at arm's-length. Cowboy shook his head with amazement at what he saw there. "I'll spend the next month of Sundays pulling all them out, but that's what nights by the campfire are for."

Pup came to stand next to Cowboy. He stared down at the man's wrist, grave concern showing on his face. Then he looked up into Cowboy's eyes. "How you going to get the little ones out?" he asked.

"My Ma always told us boys," Cowboy began. "That when nature throws some hurt at you, the good Lord often will show the blessing in it." Cowboy flicked a chunk of broken cholla stem off the slicker with the tip of his knife. Pressing it to the rock face with the toe of his boot, he sliced it lengthwise from end-to-end. The papery sheath was peeled back, exposing sticky reddish-yellow flesh. "This what the ancient people used to cure burns and cuts," he told Pup. "Can't eat it like prickly pear or saguaro, but it soothes the skin and draws out the poisons. More valuable, it dries hard as horseshoe steel."

"How's that help?" Pup asked as he watched Cowboy cover the stickers on his wrist with pulpy cholla flesh and then wrap it with his bandana.

"'Cuz in a day or so, I can snatch the dried pulp off, and the needles will go with it." Cowboy smiled at the good job he'd done with the impromptu ministrations. He turned back towards the young man and became more serious. "What got you all knotted up back there? You really think that cactus could come after you?"

For a long moment there was no answer. "Boys in the bunkhouse said that pokey-tree could fling barbs at you like it was a porcupine," Pup answered. "Fill you with enough darts, you might bleed to death."

Cowboy laughed from deep in the belly. Then he said, "And I wager they told you to keep an eye out for the seldom-seen jackalope, too." He laughed again as he saw Pup nod his head up and down with great confusion in his eyes. "Jumping Dog don't actual jump," Cowboy said. "The needles is meant to give up the cactus just as soon as the barb snags something solid, like the back of your shirt or a dogies' snout. Happens so quick, you swear that it jumped. But that's how fear is."

Pup pondered this notion but gave no response. His gaze alternated between the big man in front of him and the stand of now-broken cactus behind the outcropping.

"You been churched much back in Georgia?"

The thought of that made Pup just beam. "Oh, yes sir. I was sanctified in baptism at the Reverend Hawthorne's chapel down on Tired Creek. It was the congregation that got up the seed money for me to come west after I was orphaned."

"Then you know some Scripture," Cowboy said. "My brother Marcus is a parson over in Uvalde. He lectures me regular about fears. Says none of 'em come from the Almighty. More like, it's the sweet whispers of Satan in our ear." He watched how Pup took to that before continuing. "Brother's favorite verse on the matter is First John 4:18 'There is no fear in love. But perfect love

21

drives out fear because fear has to do with punishment. The one who fears is not made perfect in love.'"

"Not any of us are perfect," Pup protested.

"No, but God's love is, Marcus says. And I believe him." Cowboy rested a hand on the boy's shoulder. "We all fear what we don't know. That wolf didn't eat you today and the cholla didn't jump out at me. You didn't know that last night at suppertime. Now you do."

Cowboy took his time rolling the coat and slicker so that no needles were seen. He tied these back to the saddle, then petted Dusty's forehead and nose a bit before picking up the reins. "Well young pard, it's been good to cross your tracks." He stuck out his hand for Pup to shake. "You remind me of me at your age. That ain't all bad."

Once in the saddle, Cowboy reached into the top of his boot for a moment and came out with something shiny in his hand. He motioned Pup to come closer and handed it to him. "Here's a twenty dollar gold piece. Every real buckaroo should have his own set of boots made just for him. Get yourself some."

Pup took his prize with an awkward smile and a mumbled thanks. But the sincere gratitude showed in his eyes.

"Chew on this as you grow to a man, Pup -— rather I should say, Mr. Toby Guinn," Cowboy said. "The thing is: absolute fear can freeze a man where he stands, then nothing gets done. Sheer lack of it fills a man with reckless abandon, and that can get him busted up bad. With a goodly dose of righteous fear – and God's blessing - a man can live to see the next sunrise." He leaned both elbows on the saddle horn as he spoke. "I ain't scared," Cowboy said in an even tone. "But I am savvy enough to be watchful. So should you." Cowboy straightened again to secure the bonnet strings of his weathered hat beneath his chin. He turned Dusty toward the west. "*Adios, compadre.* Hope to see you on down the way."

With the sun halfway from noon to setting, Cowboy trotted Dusty back out of the valley. Together they loped the trail at an easy pace.

Their journey had begun.

Jumping Dog
Study Questions

1. Pup was afraid and unable to help Cowboy free the calf. Was he right to be afraid? Why or why not? What was a time you didn't do something because you were afraid of what might happen?

2. Cowboy commented that, "We all fear what we don't know." What are some things you don't know that you are afraid of? Are you afraid of what God might do because you don't know what he has planned? What should you do about that fear?

3. Cowboy quoted the Bible verses that say, "There is no fear in love. But perfect love drives out fear because fear has to do with punishment. The one who fears is not made perfect in love." How does God show his perfect love for you? Why would that love drive fear away?

Sam Hill

"Yee-haw, boys! Looky what I got."

Four pairs of eyes looked up from the crowded plank table. Its collection of empty tins and coffee cups were shoved off to one side in a pile. Supper in the tiny cook shack had been over for the best part of an hour. Now cards, pipes, and tobacco occupied everyone. Everyone, except the tall cowboy with the thick moustache leaning back in his chair against the wall. He sat mending Dusty's bridle with a stout knife and rawhide lacing he'd cut from mule deer skins.

The thundering commotion disturbing their peace sprang from the exuberate young puncher's sure knowledge of what he now possessed. In the hand waving above his head, Curly Harrigan held the prize cherished by any gathering of ranch hands or trail riders set down in the middle of big lonesome – an actual printed newspaper.

"A gift from the *hacendado*, the ranch boss himself." Harrigan said. "His whole family had already read it, so he give it to us. Came to him from the Western Union man in town; who took it from a conductor on the Wichita & Santa Fe in a card game last month." He smiled, showing very crooked teeth. "It's not even a year old yet."

This call for celebration began with an immediate clearing of table clutter. The broadsheet could then be viewed in full by all, with the complete decorum such an occasion demanded.

"Chai Kay Go Try *Bueña*," Harrigan started out in painful, slow phonetics, as he read the top line of bold print on the front page. A harsh voice cut him off at once.

"It says Chicago Tribune, you hopeless *tarado*. Can't you even read?" Darnell Hubbard shook his head in complete disgust. More at Harrigan's lack of dignity for this event, than for his missing literate skills. He shouldered the younger man aside, taking up the reader's position at the center of the table. It was his intention, in keeping with the time-honored custom in cattle country, to read every word on every page before they gave up this well-thumbed journal.

"Let's see where to begin here. Front page has a whole passel of choices." Hubbard's finger tapped each of the various column headings in turn. "We got the news about old General Grant going to the opera in New York City. Guess he was sober that night. Next there's a write up of this big to-do in honor of Sarah Bernhardt. And this-here's a piece about the organizing of land leagues across America — whatever that means."

He smiled as he stopped to read the next column. "Oh Lord save us," Hubbard said. "An announcement here about the first annual meeting of the National Temperance Society. Do-gooders will be the ruination of us all." For a moment, the men variously considered this warning and what it might mean before Hubbard went on. "Something here about a Panama Canal controversy. Seems rich folks are spitting at one a-tuther about who has to pay for what," he tapped the page again. "Another reports the wool sales over in London."

His finger lingered at the beginning of the article covering the bottom quarter of the front page and nearly half a column on the next. "If that don't tear it." His palm slammed flat on the paper with a thud.

"What's the matter, Hub?" Lonnie Vickers asked. "What's the rumpus?"

"It's those dern Bourbon Democrats over to the state house. Says here our Governor Roberts is plotting to get himself elected to the U.S. Senate, but dividing Texas up into four states to do it. Plans to take Reagan, Ireland, and Devine with him as the other Senators."

Harrigan and Vickers both jumped to their feet to peer over Hubbard's shoulder as he read the entire article out loud. Cowboy leaned forward in his chair, craning to read along. Only the

Englishman, whom everyone called "the Professor", remained unmoved, puffing his pipe and looking bemused at the sudden folderol.

"Sounds like that outnumbered Republican Party of Texas is on to them," Cowboy observed. "That's a burr under the horse blanket, making it no certainty."

"Maybe," Hubbard shot back. "But what the Sam Hill was he thinking?"

As thought was given to an answer for this puzzle, a deep crease furrowed across Curly Harrigan's brow. "What's this Sam Hill got to do with it?" he asked. "That hombre waddn't even mentioned in the paper." He pointed down to the Tribune.

The Professor blew out a magnificent smoke ring and said in calm tones, "Not to fret, young Harrigan. It's merely a quaint colloquialism; an expression of exasperation, actually. Something one uses when one doesn't know the proper words to employ." He puffed the pipe again with gusto, eyes twinkling.

Not satisfied, Harrigan persisted. "Well then, Professor, why use the man's name at all? And why Sam Hill? Who was he?"

"Alas, my lad, to this day that remains shockingly unclear," the Professor went on. "He might have been anyone. Care to venture your own guess?"

Harrigan stared at the man with unfocused attention, his countenance blank as he struggled to recall the people of his past. "When we was living outside Pikeville back in Kaintuck', after the Appomattox surrender, family feuds was bad. Hatfields a-gin the McCoys. Got so bloody, state militia swarmed into Pike County to bring an end to it. Cavalry officer leading them went by the name of General Samuel Ewing Hill. I remember that 'cuz I seen it on plenty of posted proclamations." He smiled at an unexpected thought that just occurred to him. "Come to think on it, every time folks would see a new decree from him they'd say 'What does the Sam Hill demand now?'" His smile spread into a grin as the notion came to him that the expression in question may have originated in his hometown.

"Not at all how I heard it, Curly," Lonnie Vickers said in boastful tones. "Growing up in Illinois, it's widespread common known that old Abe Lincoln was the reason for folks saying that.

Seems his lawyer boss back in those days was a feller named Sam Hill. A retired judge or somethin'." Vickers threw his head back as he spoke, interlacing fingers of both hands behind it – elbows out. "Story goes that Abe had penned this long set of papers about how there's nothing in the Bible 'cept what a bunch of plain folk come up with. No word of God at all. Can you imagine that?" Vickers eyes widened in disbelief even though he knew the story already. "So after reading all of it, Sam yells at Abe that he'll have no future in politics if this gets around. After that, he chucks the whole parcel into a roaring fireplace. Everything goes up in smoke."

Vickers over-exaggerated this swirling gesture with wavy hands. "Abe is all lathered up now. He tries to fetch out any unburned scrap he can reach. It's said he turns to the old man and says, 'What the…[hesitation/mumble]…Sam Hill have you done?" With a face that displayed complete lack of uncertainty, Vickers shrugged at the others around the table, palms up. "Honest Abe truth, I swear. Guess it was his way of not cussing when he'd worked up a head of steam. Kinda caught on with folks after that, when they was in similar circumstance."

"Well, you got the cussing part right," Darnell Hubbard chimed in. "But the man was from over in the Arizona Territory. A mining agent and surveyor. This Sam Hill, the real one mind you, could cuss up such a blue streak that mule skinners blushed like church goers. The Navy's sailors and even Army sergeants would steer clear of him."

Hubbard nodded his own approval of this to himself, a grave look on his face. He hardly noticed whether the others followed suit. "As a young man Sam was a pretty rough character. Working throughout the west in various and sundry occupations, he had many the adventure. Loved to tell about it in his later years, but some folks found the language a bit too salty." Hubbard looked up to meet the eyes of his table mates. "Whenever those stories got repeated in more genteel society, folks would just use Sam Hill instead of some unmentionable. And that's a fact."

When no one spoke to challenge Darnell Hubbard's tale, the Professor tapped cold ashes from his pipe into the turned up four-inch cuff of his blue jeans pant leg. He leaned forward, pressing his belly against the table. "You, sir," he directed at Cowboy, "have yet to say a word in this entire matter. Have you any insights that could be shared with the rest of us?"

The repairs now completed, Cowboy set the bridle on the table. The knife he tucked into its woven leather scabbard at his hip. For a moment he sat lips pursed together, collecting thoughts before speaking. "Can't say as I heard any of them stories before, so I got no call to say one's true and the other ain't." He looked at all of them before fixing his gaze solely at the Professor.

"I've heard folks spit out the name of Sam Hill instead of vulgarity many a time," Cowboy said. "Do so myself. I got that from my Paw." He folded both hands together on the table in the relaxed manner with which he did most things. His eyes softened as an old recollection floated up from memory. "Me and my brothers was told from time we was kids that cussing was wrong. Sinful even, if God's name was used. So Paw taught us to say Sam Hill instead." Cowboy pushed back to lean against the wall again. "Paw said it was the name of an angel, better to use it than cussing. Never thought about it any different until now."

In less time than it took anyone to blink, the Professor brought his balled fist down loudly against the rough planking, causing others to flinch. "Egad, man, your father was on to something. Surely, I should have seen this myself but I confess I've missed it." Taking up the now-empty pipe once more, the Professor sucked at it three or four times before using it to stab the air in Cowboy's direction.

"Not all that long ago, before I decided to see the wonders of this world, and the American West, I was at university. Matriculating at Christ Church College, Oxford, I read philosophy – both as a young honors student and in postgraduate studies. I dabbled in music there too; singing choir, in musicals, as well as indulging my passion for opera." He tapped the table top with the pipe stem. "Got to be quite the tenor, if I do say so. But I digress. The crux of it is that I grew very fond of continental composers, particularly the Germans. This very moment I have just remembered the great romantic masterpiece *Der Frieschütz* by von Weber." The Professor was surprised that this announcement was met by only general dumfoundedness among the gathered ranch hands.

"*Cuidado*, boys. Careful now," Darnell Hubbard said at last. "I think the Professor here is trying to sell us some sunshine."

"Not at all," the Englishman replied. "It's a fine Germanic folk tale, but no need going into all that. The point is, there's a character in it called Samiel the Black Huntsman. More to the point, this Samiel was in fact the Devil." He could see that the men, especially Hubbard were not grasping the importance of his words yet. "In my philosophy studies, you see, I read Scripture, the Talmud, and copious Hebrew and Greek. From that I learned that Samiel was one of the seven archangels." He turned to Cowboy. "So that's were your father had it right."

"How so?" Cowboy asked, one brow furled. He studied the Professor with the watchfulness of a coyote eyeing an approaching scorpion.

"My dear fellow," the Professor said. "Samiel was once the archangel who ruled the fifth heaven, only later to become the fallen angel banished to Hell's confines for eternity. He is in fact, Satan, otherwise known as Lucifer, or Beelzebub, or el Diablo as the people call him out here. Indeed, Samiel most fittingly must be this Sam Hill. Listen to the sounds: Samiel – Sam Hill. Obviously one name devolved into the other." The Professor beamed with satisfaction at this discovery. "In effect," he went on, "one is saying 'what the devil' every time one speaks his name." He smiled directly at Cowboy. "But he was an angel first, as your father correctly taught you."

Cowboy let the import of this learned man's words settle in a bit. The others huddled in stifled amazement, never had they heard such high-falootin' book-learning directed at them personally.

"My brothers will be righteous proud," Cowboy said, "when I tell 'em how you backed up Paw's belief about the angel Sam Hill. But it don't matter much what you call him, his ways are only the path of wickedness." Cowboy stood. "I only ask now as I did as a boy, 'lead us not into temptation and deliver us from evil.'"

He offered his hand to the Professor, who shook it with the genuine warmth of a kindred soul. "Take comfort in what Paul wrote to his congregates," the Professor said. "'Come together again so that Satan will not tempt you because of your lack of self control.'" Still grasping the taller man's big hand he also offered, "I expect that you'll fare ever well in that endeavor."

The newspaper was folded, placed in a suitable place of reverence for later perusal, and other preparations began for the end of a long day and the too-soon start of another.

* * *

Cowboy thanked the ranch owner and his wife for the use of an empty bunk and the fine meals he'd enjoyed over the last several weeks. "Much obliged for letting me swap cowboying your range for a new set of horseshoes for Dusty. Don't want him coming up lame, and it looks like this easy ranch life has got him fat as I've seen him." They wished him well and handed him a small cloth bundle of sourdough bread and salted sowbelly meat. It also held the pair of airtights full of peaches for that special meal somewhere down the trail.

He shook hands with the bunkhouse boys and mounted up. In a few hours' travel he was back at the trailhead. With a brief look back the way he'd come, Cowboy spurred Dusty on. For a time he listened to the sound new shoes made striking solid earth, thinking about the Englishman's words.

After some time he confessed to Dusty, "To my remembrance, I never met the devil in the actual flesh, and I pray that day never comes. Many times though, I've fallen to his temptation and given over to the ways of transgression, like some weak soul." Cowboy shook his head at the thought. "Every time, sin was made to sound so sweet and agreeable. Partly I was tricked. Mostly I knew it to be wrong, but did it just the same. A man has got to stay watchful, Dusty, against just such a crooked pathway."

With the wind at his back and the sun at his shoulder, they loped the trail together at an easy pace.

Their journey had begun.

Sam Hill
Study Questions

1. In this story, Cowboy learns that Satan was once an angel. In Isaiah, we learn that Satan's rebellion was that he wanted to take God's place and be "like the Most High." Why was it so wrong for Satan to try and be like God? What are ways you try and take over God's work in your own life?

2. How have you rebelled against God? Are you banished from heaven forever because of your rebellion, like Satan was? How is Jesus the solution for our rebellion against God?

3. The Professor quotes the Bible about having relationships with other people to help us with temptation. Who is in your life who helps you when you are tempted? How can you build a defense against temptation by connecting with others?

Trade Secrets

"Chickens ain't none too smart, Mrs. Hundley. We ought to sort this out quick enough." Cowboy watched the rancher's wife toss another handful of cracked corn to the odd assortment of hens gathered just outside the shadow of the aging barn. A dozen or so poults of different sizes and featherings busied themselves scratching the dirt for feed.

An equal number milled around the rest of the yard, more interested in soil bugs and the occasional spider. Nearby, a rooster pecked at the bottom of a cedar post -- intent on capturing something Cowboy could not see.

For several seconds, Cowboy thought about the motley gathering of poultry back on the family ranch in Atascosa County. Black ones, brown ones, red ones, speckled, and splotched. There seemed to be more of them than of the cattle. By tradition, chicken tending, egg collection, and weeding the garden was relegated to the youngest family member. First to Cowboy, then Marcus, on to Lucky, and finally to little Johnny.

Although a rite of passage to move on from herding yard birds to handling rough stock, Cowboy began to miss the daily feeds and egg hunts almost from the morning his younger brother took over. Seeing Huldah Hundley now standing in the midst of her flock, repeating clucking sounds and mouthing cooing noises, reminded him of the genuine peacefulness chickens with their constant head-bobbing jerkiness had brought him.

So it was surprising for Cowboy to consider the quandary Mrs. Hundley had presented him with. None of these beady-eyed critters had laid so much as a single egg in the last fortnight. Fed, watered, sheltered, almost pampered, and steadfastly protected from predators, they were certainly not holding up their end of the bargain.

Before Cowboy could put much thought into recalling just how he scouted for lost eggs as a boy, voices raised in anger, shouting to be heard over the other, came from just inside the barn's massive unpainted doorway.

And, although Cowboy stood some four steps closer, Mrs. Hundley tore past him and through the doors at a dead run. She didn't much cotton to disagreeable manners on her ranch – whether among her family or between the ranch hands. What she first set eyes on when entering the barn brought a flush of color to her cheeks at once.

The blacksmith, Tom Carstensen, was holding Jack Quinlan at an extended arm's length, grasping him by great handfuls of shirt and suspenders. That not withstanding, Quinlan flailed both arms like windmill blades in a cyclone, but they did little more than brush Carstensen's huge biceps and elbows. The gentle blonde Goliath from Minneapolis tightened his grip on the Irishman, determined to let Quinlan play himself out with no harm done to either of them. Bewilderment danced across his bearded face, apprehension growing, causing pale blue eyes to widen in cautious wonder. "Enough then, eh, Jack?"

"I'll not quit 'til ya give back what is me own," Quinlan spit back. He continued to thrash away with no better aim than before.

Having his back to the door and his eyes stuck on Carstensen, Quinlan did not see the two newcomers approaching the fracas. Neither did he see Mrs. Hundley draw the huge spoon out from beneath her apron that she began to wield like the sword of Gideon. But he did feel the painful result of that broad wood being applied smartly between his shoulder blades.

"Enough, you two," she said. "Stop this at once. I'll not have it on my ranch." The combatants discontinued at the sound of her voice. Begrudgingly Quinlan turned to face the woman. Both men stood quietly, heads slightly lowered, eyes not meeting hers. First graders in front of the school marm. "Jack Quinlan, I know this is your doing. You've been spoiling for a fight for more than a week now. Why, I have nary a clue."

Huldah Hundley waited in silence for an explanation. And Jack Quinlan was just bustin' to give her one.

"He's a t'ief, that one," he all but shouted, glaring at the massive blacksmith. "Took the very pewter cup me Da gave me the morning I left the Blessed Isle for this cursed Land of the Buffalo." Quinlan spat at the other man's feet. "Since that day, I've seen not a buffalo, and since Sunday last I've not seen me cup."

In that quiet moment that followed, all eyes turned to Tom Carstensen. Unruffled by the Irishman's unbridled ravings, Tom simply said, "Ma'am, I took nothing of his, cup, can, or bucket. And certainly nothing of pewter -- or diamond or gold, for that matter. I'm not that kind. I'm Lutheran."

At hearing this explanation, Quinlan whirled with surprising speed, preparing to launch himself once again into the fray. The big hand spread against his chest stopped him where he stood. Cowboy then looked down into Jack's eyes, speaking in a low but unmistakably warning tone. "Let's not we all just start shooting before the aiming's done, let's slow it down a tad."

He stepped directly between the two of them, continuing to hold Jack's gaze. "All's can be said so far, somethin' belonging to you has gone missing."

Before the Irishman could do more than gape open his mouth again, Cowboy held up his hand in front of Jack's face. "Just say more precise what it is exact we're looking for. I mean, how's it appear?"

The question seemed to stump Quinlan. It puzzled him greatly that everyone did not already know of his family's famous Leprechaun's Cup. So named by his grandmother when she bequeathed it to his father, her oldest offspring. It was passed to Jack next, in keeping with the British rule of primogeniture-- inheritance of the first born

"A wee cup, like so," Jack said. He held up a thumb and index finger about three inches apart. "Fine Celtic workmanship. The pewter's so pure, it almost shines blue."

"Cain't say as I ever seen a thing like that in my life," Cowboy replied, rubbing the knuckle of his thumb under the chin. "But I'll keep one eye open." He turned to Carstensen. "How 'bout you?" The big man just shook his head, no.

"Then we'll all give it the effort to watch out for what you're missing." Cowboy spread out his arms indicating the rancher's wife, the blacksmith and himself. "But you harness that considerable steam of yours. Instead try running to ground where it might have gone to. Start with the last place you seen it."

"Tis easy that, I..." Quinlan stopped when Cowboy stepped directly in front of him so that he had to look up to meet the wrangler's eyes.

"Perhaps I should say it more slow for you, on account of you don't know me. All your spit and clamor ain't going to find you nothing. Hard work and diligence will." Cowboy leaned in even closer to Jack. "I'll say it plain. From now on you got no proof, you throw no punches. Sabe?"

It grew quiet enough that the only sound in the barn was the milk cow in the back corner grinding jaws to chew her cud. Mrs. Hundley watched the proceedings with growing admiration. A situation that she had been unable to fathom, let alone head off, was now being handled with quiet authority by this unassuming stranger. She only hoped he knew the nature of barnyard fowls as well.

* * *

Cowboy sat back on boot heels in a comfortable half-squat. His weight balanced evenly between his two big feet dug into the soft dirt outside the barn. With his elbow resting lightly on the corral fence, he held the now lukewarm coffee cradled in the palm of his hand.

For the last three-quarters of an hour, he had made a tally, then again---checking each total against the previous count. After the third such recalculation, Cowboy was convinced that Mrs. Hundley's flock included exactly twenty-seven hens. Scratches he made in the dirt by his feet divided the birds by color or by breed as best he knew them.

But he waited still, sipping from the tin cup on occasion. Doing chores for the Hundleys was easy enough. He liked the missus. Not only could she cook, but her coffee was the best he'd ever tasted. It had something to do with the raw egg she broke into the pot just at the boiling that caught all the loose grounds and adding enrichable flavoring.

At last his patience paid off. What could only be the twenty-eighth bird, the only white bird with occasional black splotches, appeared rounding the corner of the barn. It found the feed Cowboy had piled. He'd placed it where he could see it being approached by chickens coming from any direction.

When the eating was done, the hen retraced her steps at a pace more rapid than Cowboy expected. He barely caught sight of her ducking around the feed bin, and was only barely in time to see the tips of her tail feathers disappear into an almost invisible crack between two planks in the western-most wall of the small shed.

When Cowboy studied it for a moment, he guessed that if he hadn't a seen it himself, he wouldn't have thought a chick could have squeezed through that gap, let alone some adult fowl.

The stout wooden latch, held in place by dried strips of cow leather tacked to the door, did not move at Cowboy's touch. Not until he put his strength into it, did the wood slide free enough to open the shed. Not a door much used, he calculated.

The shed's interior combined hand tools in bad need of mending, crates stacked with empty preserve jars, rolls of fencing wire, and an assortment of items Cowboy could not identify at first glance. The sudden sunlight and whoosh of fresh air that burst into that tiny space, on the heels of the unexpected tall human set off a cacophony of noise and agitation. More than a dozen chickens flapped wings angrily at the intruder, while still seeming to run in all directions at once. Cowboy had to laugh. "*Mitotes del Pollo,*" he said under a big grin. And, indeed they were a doing a very wild chicken dance.

Enough light poured into the shed so that Cowboy could count at least ten eggs pyramiding into a pile in the midst of a fence coil. The empty crates were over-strewn with hay and live oak leaves, only partially covering eggs left behind. Each corner sported its own nest.

Cowboy had figured right. Some recent threat caused the chickens to seek out a new roost that gave them more privacy and made them feel safe. They hadn't stopped laying, just stopped laying where they used to. Mrs. Hundley would be surprised, but relieved. He knelt down on one knee to inspect the nest made in an overturned nail barrel. Barely room enough for a full sized hen and her brood.

As he hefted himself to stand, Cowboy's eye's caught sight of another hidey-place. But this one was a good three feet off the dirt, lodged between the two braces that supported the chest-high shelf which ran the length of one wall. He stared at it a bit before judging it much too small for a chicken. Carefully stepping around the boxes and wire in his path, Cowboy was at last able to stare into its opening. Too dark to see much inside until he fired up a sulphur-tipped match from his vest pocket.

A menagerie of items clustered in there, some even sparkled in the dim glow. But the opening was too small for his hand. "Well darn if it ain't a wood rat," he said, nodding his head in agreement with his conclusion. "Didn't know they ventured this far south -- or east." He took the knife from its sheath on the back of his belt. Using it and a light from a second match, he managed to scrape out the odd contents of the nest into the palm of his hand.

A broken china cup's fine handle caught Cowboy's eye. Its glaze still dazzled. He set that aside before taking up the next, a stitcher's thimble of hardened steel. Its row upon row of dimpled gnarls festooned the shiny surface. Cowboy could but barely fit it atop his little finger.

The remaining items contained a cavalcade of bits and pieces. Most notable among them, a short length of satin ribbon, three small snags of calico cloth, and a black button cracked nearly in half.

Cowboy stepped back toward the light of the shed's doorway, stopping a good two feet shy of the sill. He stood there to examine the contents still in his palm. From the corner of his eye, he could see Jack Quinlan slink past the barn, carrying an ax handle recently carved of green wood. Quinlan held it along the length of his leg so as to make it less visible. Cowboy judged this was done not for any peaceful purpose.

He jammed the little treasures into the pocket of his range coat, and took after Quinlan. The shorter man stopped about three feet behind the bent over figure of Tom Carstensen who busied himself clanging a two pound hammer against the anvil, forging a length of metal into some particular shape. The noise was deafening, as evidenced by the rolled bandana circling the big man's forehead and covering his ears before being tied at the back of the head. Tom could not have heard bellowing cows right behind him through all that din.

Quinlan raised the ax handle above his head as though to strike the smithy in twain with a single blow. Instead, Cowboy's grip upon Jack's collar together with the decided jerk towards the ground, felled the Irishman like a steer bulldogged into the dirt. A boot heel ground into the fallen man's chest.

"I see you ain't thrown off the scent easy, once you get to tracking. But what you were about to do is bad wrong," Cowboy said. "You got a quarrel with a fella, be a man and take it to his face. Don't sneak up on the blind side like some cussed yokel with no morals."

Cowboy blew out a big sigh, disgust in his eyes. "The Devil himself would shake his head at your cowardice. Where's the honor in cold-cocking someone? That path leads only to regret, a mighty tough thing to share your slumber with."

Quinlan struggled to raise himself. Cowboy eased him back down with the boot. "This cup's got you all eat up with loco. Sorry as hang. Unrighteous anger makes a fool of a man. Why's it so doggone important?" he asked. "Let the cup go until your mind is right. It's just some thing."

"I canna let it go. Don't you see?" Quinlan whined. "It's all the meaning in the world to me."

With his foot still square on the other's chest, Cowboy bent to retrieve the ax wood. He balanced it in one hand, judging the heft. He ran a thumb along the cut edges, and finally sniffed the fragrance of the fresh cedar it had been hewn from. Looking down, he tapped the tip of the wood against Quinlan's arm near the shoulder. "Would the cup mean as much to you if someone was to bash your head in the way you was about to do Tom?"

Tears were Quinlan's only reply for almost a minute. Carstensen stood by unmoving, perplexed by this turn of events. But he knew better than to interfere. "Twas the only thing left of me family," the Irishman sobbed. "Many's the time I watch me Gran use it with needle and thread to darn socks and such. And sew the dresses for me four little sisters. Then me mum as well, giving up the whale bone sliver she used on her finger to sew until the cup was passed to us."

"What?" Cowboy said in half-exasperation. "You mean this?" In a second of fumbling he dug the thimble from his coat pocket, showing it to Jack.

"Saints be praised," Quinlan shouted. "Wherever did this come to ye?" He grasped the object along with Cowboy's hand in both of his, kissing the collected mound of flesh with lips wet from his slobbering.

Cowboy shook him loose before holding the thimble up for Carstensen to see. The wrangler's face darkened as he stared at it. "This?" he said to Quinlan. "This was worth the blood you were about to spill, the man you was about to tump? This bit of common house goods?" With his free hand he jerked Quinlan to his feet. "This ain't a cup, and it plain sure ain't even pewter. What in the world were you going on about?"

"Sure, and I stretched the truth a wee bit about the metal. It was for the leprechauns, you see." Quinlan shrugged. "It wouldn't do to let them know we were so poor that we could only afford that made of steel."

"And it being a cup?" Cowboy asked. His eyes narrowed as he continued to hold Quinlan by the collar.

"Oh, 'tis a cup if you think about it. The leprechauns have tiny wee hands, you see. Each eve me Da would fill it with whisky, and next morn 'twould all be gone. Da claimed 'twas the little people that had drunk it." Quinlan shrugged again and eased himself out of Cowboy's grip. "When the whisky ran out, so did the luck. I set out for America after that." He took the thimble in his own hand, examining it with great satisfaction. "Ye dinna say, how came you by it? It went missing afore ye ever rode up to the ranch."

Recovered enough from his incredulousness, Cowboy brought out the handful of items he'd taken from the crowded nest. "You was visited by a pesky rodent known widely as the wood rat. Some folks call it the pack rat. Likes trinkets. Also likes to do himself one better when he can." Cowboy picked out the button from his hand. "Might have started out hunting to find what he could find.

Picks up something shiny like this button and heads back to the nest. Along the way he comes across something even shinier -- like your thimble. Takes it instead, and leaves the button. Figures it's an even trade. Even if he done it in secret, without you knowing." He looked at Carstensen, who seemed to consider the notion, then he looked back at Quinlan.

"Aye and now you mention it, at the very spot I last laid me cup I found a wee glass bead. Curious it was, but I was too flummoxed to pay it no never mind." He grinned wildly at the thimble in his hand, but became somber as he looked up into Tom Carstensen's face. "It's you I've done grievously. I canna say how sorry 'tis that I am. Me going off with threats and such other as I couldna justify." Jack licked his lips twice before going on. "May be will nay be friends, but let's now neither be enemies. The fault 'tis mine alone."

Tom Carstensen responded by placing a big paw of a hand on each of Jack's shoulders and shaking him playfully. Then he nodded several times, smiling. But he spoke no words aloud.

Quinlan turned at last to Cowboy, relief etched on his face. "What caused ye to take such interest in the likes of us and our wee tiff? This fight meant something to you, but I canna ken why. We're but strangers."

Carstensen spoke at last. "I'd say it was personal and very much so. Am I wrong?"

Cowboy smiled, but the grin did not reach his eyes. "Meant what I said about living with regret born out of quarrelsomeness. Can get so's you think about it with each sunrise, and most nights when you close your eyes to the stars above." He sat down on an overturned wooden bucket, resting hands on his knees.

"My Pa became a winter parson after getting the Gospel call in his later years. Heard some Bible-thumping sermonizer at a tent revival down in Nueces. Forever changed his life -- and ours. Being a preacher's boy then, I was expected to be mild-tempered all the time. The local banker was *muy rico*; a rich man. Every rancher in the county owed him money of some amount. But he had this no-account fatso kid. That yahoo fancied himself quite the bully. Begins this tussle with me, mocking that I had to turn the other cheek if I was to be true to the Scriptures. Then swings at me like some drunk washer woman. He missed. I didn't. I hit his cheek so hard that it loosed some teeth and busted a jaw. Had to tell him he'd mistaken me for my little brother, the one that took the Sermon on the Mount more to heart than I had. I set out to the trail drives a week after that with my Pa's blessing and my Ma's tears.

Cowboy studied his boot a moment. "Last thing I heard my Pa tell me was, 'Blessed are the peacemakers, for they shall be sons of God.' I thought of that, and the fatso with the busted face, all the way to Kansas behind nine-hundred foul-smelling cattle. It hurt all the more on account them words is from Mathew."

"Why is that?" Jack Quinlan asked.

"Because it came first," Cowboy answered evenly. "First of the four Gospels."

* * *

"Sure you won't take up the offer to stay?" Huldah Hundley asked Cowboy. "My husband could really use your help."

"No ma'am," the wrangler replied. "I do believe he can manage on his own."

"Didn't expect so," she said. "You have this look in your eye. It's not something you're looking for, nor someone either. It's more like there's some place you've got to be."

Cowboy managed a weak smile, but said nothing.

"I hope you get there," she said. "And that it's the place you should be going."

They shook hands briefly before Cowboy mounted Dusty. He spurred the big horse to a trot until they came to the trail they'd been traveling. South took them toward Camp Verde and Kerrville, north to San Saba. Cowboy studied the southern path. His heart tugged him that way. But his head knew he was not ready. He turned Dusty north.

They loped the trail together.

Their journey had begun.

Trade Secrets
Study Questions

1. Jack was focused on revenge, even though he
    didn't know all the facts. Have you ever tried to
    take revenge without enough information? What
    should we do instead? Even if you knew someone
    wronged you, is taking revenge ever a right
    response? Why or why not?

2. Tom was willing to forgive when Jack apologized.
    Cowboy was still pondering a wrong he did long
    before. How should we resolve disputes like
    these? What should your response be when
    someone asks for forgiveness? What things have
    you done to others that require you to seek
    forgiveness?

3. Jesus said that peacemakers are blessed. What
    does it mean to be a peacemaker? How is Jesus the
    example of someone who made peace between
    God and us? How can you do the same for people
    around you?

PART 2

Rendezvous

A Word Given

"Ray's dead."

Those few words, and the long silence that followed, were all the warning Cowboy got that his old friend had unexpectedly passed over. That jolt of ill tidings staggered the wrangler. Like being sucker-punched hard in the ribs, Cowboy found it tough to draw next breath. He felt his insides clench up, gripped by some unseen hand. For many years Ray Patterson, in close partnership with his pretty wife Esmeralda, had owned the tidy boarding house next door and that white-washed horse barn, in which Cowboy was now standing holding Dusty by the reins. The buildings sat squat on the rise just before the trail went down into Cowtown.

Cowboy guessed the man staring back at him stone-faced and still as a monument was the current, albeit much less affable, proprietor. "His woman sold me this place four days after they put him in the ground," the man said. "Then I heard she went back to her people in New Mexico, somewhere near that big pueblo east of Santa Fe."

The old man resembled an aging Percheron stallion: barrel of a chest, thick through the belly, and stout across the haunches. Thin white hairs of uneven length poked out from the brim of his snap-brim hat. "Folks 'round here complain I speak too plain," he said. But Cowboy heard no apology in his voice. "Don't mince," the man continued. "Just say what I say straight-forward. On occasion," he begrudged, "wife calls it hurtsome and rude. Took you for just another drifter about to tell me some hard luck yarn about life in the saddle and trying to natter a free meal out of me.

49

And some feed for his horse, too." The man's protruding lip indicated how unlikely that would be. "Name's John Dowling." The man did not extend his hand to the tall stranger. Instead, he stood flatfooted, struggling to match Cowboy's unflinching gaze. "That look on your face just now," the man said at last. "Patterson must have meant something to you. He kith or kin?"

Words did not come to Cowboy the first time he tried. He had to swallow hard, twice, just to wet his mouth enough to speak. "Ray and me was pards from way back" Cowboy answered in a tone too weak to be characteristic of him. "First time I ever pushed cattle north from Texas, he was the only drover in the outfit to take me under his wing. I was still just a boy compared to them other punchers, but Ray kept me from hurting myself when I'd do something stupid with the beeves or the horses." Cowboy felt a rush of warmth roll down his neck and back recalling those many foibles. "Truth be told, I owe that man my life, on more than one occasion."

"When you last seen him?" Dowling asked, ignoring the Texan's brief struggle with reminiscence and grief.

"Three years come August," Cowboy said, composed once more. "Last time I brought a herd across the Pedernales. Stayed here two days. He seemed fit as a yearling then."

"Boarding house not the place I'd expect a passel of trail hands to bed down, when the lures of Cowtown are so close."

"Oh, I'd visit Ray and Essie, as he called her, while the boys whooped it up in town after the cattle sold and we got our money."

"Put you up with the paying boarders did he?"

Cowboy imagined that if Dowling had been wearing a money belt around his ample bib-and-brace dungarees at that moment, he'd be clutching it close. Using both hands. "Not like that at all," he said. "The lone place I ever slept on this whole property is in that hayloft behind you." Cowboy pointed over Dowling's head. "And that was only after Ray'd worked me hard enough to earn leftover vittles from that day's table fare. Once't, I pitched a wagon's worth of silage into that loft in the span of an afternoon. Another, I cut a whole load of saw-milled lumber to length so we could put up that shed out back. Last time, I shimmied up the windmill tower to replace two broken blades and unbend that crooked throw rod. Made Essie's cooking taste that much better." Cowboy slid into another fond reverie at the thought of her. "Ham and biscuits were my favorite. That lady could cook anything from scratch."

Cowboy turned away from Dowling now. He took the time to sweep his look across the barn in all directions. Stalls had been recently cleaned, but not today. Tack and equipment hung in place by rows. And the only two bags of feed stood stacked squarely in a corner. This, Cowboy judged, was work done by other hands. Dowling's clean finger nails and unsoiled clothing suggested that, but his hat's absence of sweat stains confirmed it. Without question, the man seemed to wheeze with every word spoken, more deeply even with the mildest exertion. And though Dowling disguised it with a fresh juniper sliver clenched between his teeth, the sourness of some fermented brew wafted over Cowboy every time the man spoke.

"Ain't seen your hired man since I rode up today," Cowboy said. "What manner of chore you got him on?"

"Not a thing." Dowling replied. His lower lip thrust out once more, this time joined by the thick upper one as well. He held his face as though sucking a lump of lemon sour candy. "He's gone. Lit out this morning, right after I paid his wage. Wasn't long after he read that letter I handed him, along with the money, that he yelled out, 'Oh Caroline' and threw his few belongings in an old war bag. Minutes later, he'd saddled that skinny pony of his and galloped out of town, headed north." Dowling stared at the toes of his work boots. "Like as not, I've seen the last of Billy Mitchell."

At this unexpected turn of events, Cowboy nodded—more to himself than to Dowling. "See-ins you're a man short and still got chores aplenty, I say we parlay. There's a wagon's load of uncut timbers outside needs chopped to firewood. I don't for the life of me see you doing that yourself."

"Give you same arrangement as Ray did, I guess: loft for a bed and meal fixin's every day," the old man said with a straight face.

"Naw," Cowboy replied. "I don't owe you same as I done him." His eyes began to twinkle. "Looks like Billy Mitchell give you good effort in all he done. What deal was it you strike with him?"

"Same as I just said," Dowling replied. "Except five U.S. dollars paid in coin at each month's end." He bit his jaws hard together after he spoke, almost but not quite managing to make his eyes go neutral.

"Looks like that deal couldn't keep him here," Cowboy said. "You'd sooner catch rattlesnakes eating from berry bushes than see me work for such little as that." He smiled, and took his time folding the leather gloves in his hand before shoving them into a coat pocket. "No matter. I'll stay to Sunday next, do what needs doing in the barn. I'll split your wood and stack it too. Cost you three dollars plus that other." He shifted his weight toward Dowling. "Fair enough?"

Dowling nodded one time without hesitation, punctuating the agreement with a loud harrumph. He took two steps to go around Cowboy on the way to the boarding house, when Cowboy stopped him. "I was brought up to handshake a deal when it's struck. Let the other fella know, when you look him in the eye, that you'd keep your word." He held his big hand out to Dowling.

The old man, for his part, moved in closer and raised a thick palm to his face. With a pop of dry air from his puckered mouth, Dowling pretended to spit in his hand and shook Cowboy's. As Dowling stepped back, tall puncher asked him, "You must be Amish?"

"Was," Dowling said and walked out of the barn.

The balance of the afternoon allowed the time for Cowboy to ease himself from trail rider back to a working hand once more. He unsaddled Dusty, throwing the blanket, rig, and bridle over the wood of the closest stall. Cowboy took his time with the groom's brush he'd found, giving the horse's neck, back, and legs a thorough going-over. He spent extra time brushing any spot matted down by sweat and rubbing leather. Then Cowboy settled into to doing Dowling's work, starting with the stalls.

Not that the choice mattered much, Cowboy found himself once again humming a long forgotten ditty from his childhood. "Green Grow the Lilacs" now was mostly sung by the old-timers, particularly those who believed that song begat the term "gringo". The Professor had once assured Cowboy the name actually started in Spain, and besides Cowboy was rarely called that name to his face any more. His most immediate concern was where to put the horse droppings he'd finished raking into a small heap. The compost pile Ray carefully maintained out back had disappeared. Essie had used it with such success in her tidy cottage garden. Weeds and rabbit grass now stood in place of her herbs and tomatoes.

In one breath, then two, and finally a third, Cowboy recognized that some new scent had swirled around him on the breeze. The wind blew through the double doors facing to the east, made its way across the barn's length, before funneling out through a set of Dutch windows high on the back wall. Now, mixed with the smell of hay and horse manure, he could detect a distinct whiff of roses. Cowboy could remember that bouquet in particular from the big clump of yellow ones in front of his home place in Atascosa County. His mother pampered them there every spring.

Turning where he stood with pitchfork in hand, Cowboy stopped when he saw the girl. Eighteen years he guessed, and recognized that she would be quite the beauty in her majority. She stood tallish. Long braids hung bound together by a thin slip of lace. They swept around the neck and down one shoulder, dangling past her apron's top. The dress of threadbare calico matched her well-worn leather footwear. But the apron appeared, to Cowboy, to center her utmost attention and pride. A homespun cloth extending past the knees, it easily stretched across the narrow hips. Along its edges, hand-sewn threads were needled into floral decoration, with the most elaborate embellishments looping across the apron's bib. Such stitching evidenced a talented skillful woman. One with much time on her hands.

Cowboy did not see the resemblance in her face, but asked just the same, "You old man Dowling's daughter?"

"For a fact, I am not," she said. Her eyes, a watchful pecan-brown, held Cowboys own in a stare that seemed to bore right through him. It held an equal mix of caution and curiosity. "Lydia Dowling, currently his wife, is my mother's oldest sister. I'm Emma Sanford." She closed the gap between them by taking three small strides. "And who, sir, might you be?"

Her direct dealing and steadfast manner made Cowboy like this Emma instantly. In one hand she held a tin plate full of dumplings and some side meat and in the other a folded cloth

53

containing small chunks of day-old bread. He could smell those too, now that she was close.

"Guess best way's said, I'm the new man been given charge of barn, stock, and feed. Stalls got my attention to begin with, as you can see from this pile."

"New?" she burst the question at him. "What have you done with Billy Mitchell?"

"Can't say, miss. Never laid eyes on him myself. Only heard tell." Cowboy set the pitchfork aside and squared himself to watch the girl more fully. Her face had begun to flush in some agitation. "From what old Dowling spoke of this morning," Cowboy continued, "it seems the fella throws kit and kaboodle across a horse and hightails it outta here in one big sweat."

With a calmness that masked her growing unease, Emma placed the tin and cloth atop a stout wooden bin at her feet. She all but brushed Cowboy out of her way as she hurried to the tack room door at the barn's rear corner. It opened on noisy dead-nail hinges.

Sixty long seconds of fretful silence, Emma stood in the shadowed doorway, one hand on the jamb, the other clinging the latch. In the afternoon's failing light, she could feel more than see the room's emptiness of everything Billy Mitchell. Gone was the bedroll from the narrow cot. Gone too were jacket and denims once hung on a cedar peg. No folded razor, no pocket watch on the shelf; just gathered ranch implements and leathers left behind when Ray's wife sold out to Emma's uncle.

Cowboy stood without a word, watching the girl's head shake slowly side to side, chin to her chest. He had no sister, and at this age no daughter, to judge the pain and disappointment he now was a witness to. Like watching a crippled calf being swarmed by coyotes, his heart began to pain.

She re-closed the flimsy door. To its rough uneven surface she spoke out low, "Billy Mitchell, you are a weakling and a liar." No tears fell; only the muffled choke of her hard swallow could be heard before she went on. "You broke the one promise you swore you'd always keep."

In such a disposition, Emma turned to see Cowboy as if for the first time. She quickly recovered, but defeat still clung to her pretty features. To him she said, "You're doing the work now, so I suppose that supper's yours. Leave the plate on the stoop and I'll see you get fed breakfast too." In a moment she was through the barn's huge open doors.

"Evening, Miss Sanford," Cowboy told the retreating figure, touching his hat's brim. Bringing his full attention then to the still empty tack room compartment he said, "Billy Mitchell, I pray our paths shall cross one day soon." Fingers of one big hand tightened to a ball. "I have a fist full of uncried tears to bring you, *su cobarde*. You coward. Then maybe your tally page in Emma's ledger won't be so deep in the hole."

He flipped the cloth back on the bundle sitting next to the plate. Taking the largest chunk of darkened bread, Cowboy walked to Dusty's stall. The horse had watched the goings-on as well, his head and neck extended over the stall's short gate. Cowboy fed the piece to Dusty and stroked the ears while thinking still of Billy. "The boy was reared all wrong, *compadre*," he said. "Living out here a man should know, for any pard you'd trust to ride the river with, keep your word above all else. That's even in the Bible."

* * *

The air stayed cool that morning even under a cloudless sky. Sun had just begun to filter over the tops of Dowling's house and barn. But, Cowboy could begin to feel a warmer trace that would only increase along these rolling plains in coming days.

He sat leaned back against the buckboard's box seat. One boot rested propped against the brake handle. Cowboy seldom wasted time. Even as he sat waiting for the ladies of the house, he pulled the hardback from his coat and began to read.

Both horses of his team stood silent, with little movement, in their leather collar and tugs. Occasionally, one or the other would give its hide a shake, bob and snort, or paw at some rock in the dirt with a hoof.

Through the curtained window nearest him, the one facing out across the covered porch, Cowboy heard the mantle clock begin to chime the coming hour. Before the count came halfway done, Emma Sanford stepped through the door. Cowboy grinned on the inside. He'd already judged her to value timeliness as much as she did the detail of her sewing.

The book he jammed back in his coat pocket, finding that it almost didn't fit on the first try. "Morning, miss," Cowboy said with a touch of the hat, as he slid from seat to ground. He extended his palm up, for her to use or not, as she reached for the mounting step. Emma took his hand. "And to you, sir," she said, flashing a smile that verged on true merriment. She caught him glancing at the door with puzzled anticipation as he untied the team from their weighted horse tether.

When Cowboy did not immediately return to his post on the wagon seat, Emma said, "My aunt's not coming, if that's what you're waiting for. She doesn't feel well. It will be just you and me this morning." So, Cowboy clambered into the wagon beside her and unwound the reins from the brake handle.

He saw the smile again and thought how different that looked from her expression just two nights ago, the last time he'd actually seen her. Her dress was different, too. Just as old as the other; grey not calico. No apron, but a small bonnet sat atop her upswept hair, held there by a substantial hat pin of some antiquity. Cowboy judged it to be a valued heirloom. Its length was that or longer than the knife he wore sheathed at his hip.

"Are you always so formal?" She asked.

"Tradition, miss." Cowboy agreed. "Leastwise, the way Ma raised us boys. Proper conduct when ladies was present." He let that hang.

"She did a fine job," Emma said. "Which is more than I can say for my own kin. Today, you carry an unchaperoned young woman of a certain age to the heart of the ill-reputed Cowtown and return her home." She stopped only to catch her breath. "By yourself mind you. So either they trust you without question, having known you less than three days – or perhaps they think I'm not worth the worry."

Cowboy studied Emma's features before reply. He began to smile. "I 'spect with your frank speaking and direct manner, you're more likely to air out a man's liver two or three times with that stout silver pin of yours than put up with anything untoward." His smile broadened. "Comes down to it, miss, I'm the one needs protecting here."

That drew her laughter. "I swear I won't stick you if you'll just call me Emma."

Cowboy let the horses bump the wagon along at an easy gait. "Sorry to hear your aunt's feeling so poorly. It's a fine day for a ride in the fresh air."

"W-e-l-l," Emma exaggerated that one syllable. "Today, she has the vapors, or is it her lumbago? I can't remember." She shrugged with the slightest movement of her shoulders. "It might be that dyspepsia again or maybe the gout. No, wait, that was last week. Doesn't matter. Whatever the infirmity, it seems to keep her chair-bound most of the day, leaving all the cleanup and cooking to me." She looked at Cowboy with widened eyes filled with false earnestness. "She does, however, manage to recover in time to sit at the table for mealtime."

An unseen rut caught a lead wheel hard enough to jerk the wagon sideways. The two passengers pitched in their seats, bouncing them together. Cowboy slapped the reins hard to keep the rig from bogging down in the rough patch.

"If you don't mind my asking, Emma," Cowboy ventured. "They're not your maw and pa, so why are you living here? Have your folks passed on?"

"No," Emma answered. "That was just the first betrayal. More and more I find that people don't keep their word." She dared him with her look. "Do you?"

Without taking his eyes off the road or the team, Cowboy simply said, "A word given is a promise kept." He turned to find Emma watching him intently. He said, "What double-dealing have you endured?"

"After they bought the place, my aunt and uncle found that it was more than they could handle. My parents sent me here to lend a hand until they could settle in and find good help. 'A year at most they said.' That was almost three years ago." Her jaw set more in determination than resignation. "My entreaties to my folks have been answered only with equivocation. So, I'm left to cook and clean and sew. I'd call that a broken promise."

"You said 'first'. Were there others?" Cowboy asked.

"Uncle John and Aunt Lydia told me that I would be just like the daughter they never had. We'd be as close as my real family."

That thought produced a half-smile. "Indentured servitude should have ended when General Washington defeated the Redcoats, but I'm living proof that it's still alive and well. A second promise shattered."

"How's Billy Mitchell figure into all this?" Cowboy asked.

"He's just the latest." Her tone turned flat. "Knew when he said it, he didn't mean it. Billy swore that when he finally left this place, he'd take me with him." She gave a weak laugh. "It still hurt when he left alone. A promise is a promise."

And still no tears came. Emma looked out at the uneven wave of open prairie, absent of any trees too tall. But her eyes focused on nothing. She said, "Folks breaking a promise are lying to you, but not to your face. Like being cut with a knife, except you don't feel the pain 'till the betrayal comes to light. Hard to trust anyone after enough of them do it, especially family." She looked at her hands for a moment. "I don't know which is worse, the fact that the promise was a lie or that I believed them."

After a pause Cowboy asked, "You figure to marry Billy, or just take up with him?"

"Not like that at all." Emma said a bit more lively. "He wanted to go back to Littlefield, where he came from, once he'd gotten over this girl who broke his heart. Said he could work in the feed store there. Since I'm good with figures, I could get on with the bank or I could cook at the railroad café." She looked at Cowboy with impish eyes. "You didn't tell me about the letter Billy got or mention this Caroline. No wonder he left in such haste. I was just dirt on his boots."

For long moment the only the rhythmic grating of the kingbolt holding the harness fast to the wagon and the accompanying creak of seat springs broke the silence.

"When I peeked out the curtains, just before the clock rang, I saw you reading something. What was it, a dime novel or some penny western?" She asked.

"No, miss, it was my Bible."

"You're a Christian then?" Emma asked as though she'd never seen one this close up before.

"Mostly," Cowboy responded.

"I thought you either were or you weren't. What makes you say it that way?"

"I got a younger brother, Marcus," Cowboy said. "Who's a preacher back home. Has the faith like no man I ever seen. Couldn't bend it with railroad steel." His eyes filled with wonder at the thought of it. "I'm not there yet. Truth is, I don't give it my full attention. And there are things I got to work out in my mind first." He looked relieved to tell her. "Sorta why me and Dusty are headed up the trail. Something I got to do first."

Emma saw the brown leather corner jutting out from the coat pocket. "Where would I read in there about promises being kept?" She pointed to the book.

"You tell me," Cowboy said. He wrestled out the hardback and handed it to her as he spoke. "I'll be sure to get it back when I take my leave, end of the week. Till then, it's yours to read over. Start wherever you will and give it a go."

Emma looked at the book now in her lap like it was some flat-tailed horny toad, but she made no protest. Neither did she give it back.

Before more could be said, Cowboy reined in the horses at the town limit sign. Cowtown had changed some since his last visit, more mercantile stores than he remembered. "Where should I let you off?" He asked. "Won't take that long for me to load up your uncle's freight delivery at the depot. Be back before you know it."

Emma directed him to the large store standing in the midst of a long block of wooden buildings. She took a paper from her dress pocket and patted the coins in there. It was part of her ritual that began the coming haggle with shopkeepers over the list of goods she needed. This was the sheer pleasure in her otherwise monotonous living.

* * *

The bustle of the big city did not sit well with Cowboy's contemplative nature. Throngs of townspeople, numbering as many as three abreast, crossed the rutted street in front of the buckboard carefully stepping around manure mounds. They all seemed to be talking at once, each voice raised to be heard over the others. The number of mounted riders making their way to and fro, bound for places Cowboy could not fathom, greatly exceeded that needed to push any large herd from here to Montana. Their shouts to one another only added to the general din. The quantity of buggies, surreys, shays, and carts was more than Cowboy cared to count. Cowtown was anything but quiet.

The clamor only increased as Cowboy and his team neared the train station with the freight depot nearby. Metal striking metal around the locomotive, wood on wood as freight boxes were shoved along the loading dock. Cowboy longed for the stillness of the trail, where the only sound was the blowing wind and Dusty's footfalls on the ground. He waited with reins in hand for a somewhat large freight wagon, stacked high with oak barrels lashed together, to leave the loading dock. Four pair of stout horses strained and puffed to pull that load.

Cowboy saw that his mild annoyance with the city sounds was more that matched by the wiry grey pony a young man was struggling to tie to a hitching post in front of the depot office. Ears back flat, eyes darting wildly, the horse jerked hard at the reins in an effort to get himself away from there - to no avail. Cowboy judged the young rider to be quite the horseman, if he had the boldness to bring such an excitable animal into all this commotion. The man carried himself well, had handsome strong features, and seemed dressed neither exactly for town or for the trail. He soon disappeared through the office door.

Cowboy eased the team up to the platform. "Sent to get a parcel shipped to John Dowling," he said as he handed the freight man paperwork given to him by the old man. He was rewarded with a small but particularly heavy wooden crate. It took all the efforts Cowboy and two railroad men could muster to heave the freight into the wagon. Stenciled to the top in bold black paint was the name "Plymouth Iron Windmill Company—Plymouth, Michigan."

Having thanked the depot men, Cowboy stood next to the wagon wiping sweat from his face with a huge red bandana. He thought for a moment how little help Dowling would be getting this box to the ground once he carried it back home. The consolation Cowboy hoped for was that Emma would cook another boggy top pie for supper. Dessert was not in his arrangement with Dowling, but Emma still snuck him a fresh cut of each new pastry.

The young owner of the grey pony nodded to Cowboy as he untied the horse's leathers. Cowboy nodded in return, but was really trying to decide whether he favored Emma's egg custard or her deep dish cinnamon apple concoction. He only needed to stop for her and her few purchases, and make the easy trek home in the squeaky buckboard.

It was not to be.

Cowboy marveled to watch a few events confluence to produce such incredible tumult. It took less than a single second.

First, the locomotive fireman pulled the lever to release the steam brake's hold on the front wheels. Escaping boiler pressure produced a hissing cloud that swirled in a rush onto the tracks. The accompanying heat was hot enough to make even the most ardent non-believer shout, 'there is a Hell'.

Second, the engineer tugged the chain, emitting an ear-splitting blast from the pudgy brass whistle. The reverberation, coming from so near, set Cowboy's teeth on edge.

Third and last, that combined cacophony might as well have been the starter's pistol beginning a horse race. The grey pony took six fast strides on a wild path directly away from the frightening racket.

The rider pulled the reins hard, one leather in each hand. He tried to stop the horse or at least slow him down. That didn't work. Instead, the pony began to crow hop, punctuated by erratic kicks of both hind legs. Unable to throw the rider from his back, the pony whirled back the way they'd come. He sprinted toward a narrow alleyway. Wooden signs, low-hanging beams, and cantilevers made passage on horseback questionable. The pony determined to use those obstacles, instead of a tree limb, to scrape the man off the saddle.

Cowboy stepped into their oncoming path, shrugging off his coat as he did so. That he threw over the horse's eyes and ears with his left arm. Then he jumped up to encircle the pony's neck with his right. Feet splayed, Cowboy dug his boot heels hard into the dirt. He inched fingers up the horse's mane until he could find the desired spot. Just behind the ears, near where neck bones meet the skull, nerve pathways bundle. With his thumb, Cowboy could feel it beneath the horsehide. He mashed with all his strength.

Immediately, it had the wanted effect. The pony began to slowly circle toward the direction of the thumb. He also began to bob his head up and down as though counting. Almost at once he went buck-kneed and wobbly; legs spreading until the chest nearly touched the ground.

"Get off," Cowboy shouted over his shoulder to the rider. "And stand clear."

The man needed no second instructive. He was to the dirt next to Cowboy before the pony drew another breath.

With the horse still blindfolded, and now disoriented, Cowboy threw a stirrup over the seat. He unbuckled the cinch and shoved the saddle off with the flat of his hand. The pony began to recover a bit. Cowboy grabbed the bridle's cheekpiece. "What'd you pay for this useless fuzztail?" he asked. "More than ten dollars, and you was hoodwinked."

"The fellow had a whole string of them," the man said. "Got him for five".

Hearing that, Cowboy loosed the throat latch behind the horse's jaw. He jerked his coat clear of the pony's face and slid the bridle off. Freed once more, the horse scallyhood away, fast enough to beat the Dutch. He ran to the open country just north of the depot.

Cowboy shook the dust from his coat before putting it back on. "I'm John Calvin Quinn," the young man said. He stuck his hand out. "But folks most call me Cal. I owe you much thanks, mister." His voice had the edge of tremor in it. Cowboy shook and nodded, but said nothing. He noticed that the man's grip quivered ever so slightly. No other outward sign of the man's brush with certain harm evidenced itself in his manner.

Uncomfortable with the silence, Cal then asked, "What do they call you?"

This direct lack of manners brought a near-smile from Cowboy. "Call me the one who knows horse flesh a lot better than you do." Without being asked, he put the man's saddle and bridle into the back of his wagon, next to the freight box. "Reckon you'll be needing another goose-rumped colt now that your pony's gone.

Let me carry you to the livery other side of town." He bent to pick up a stick from the ground. With it, he began to scrape the caked dirt from the bottom of his boots. "I noticed that pony was fierce nervous when I brought the team up to the depot. Didn't like being tied to that post, with all that city clamor around him." Cowboy tossed the muddy stick back where he found it.

"What makes a horse that way? Cal asked.

"He had that look," Cowboy said. "Best I figure, he was a lightning-spooked horse. Most are kilt when the bolt strikes. Some are singed bad, others burnt something awful. Ones like yours just stay skittish all their lives." He nodded to himself as well as Cal, "Better off in the wild."

They both stood. Cal looked around this unfamiliar locale. "I'm not a man to pull a cork, or I'd buy you a drink," he said. "When I want to refresh myself, or steady my spirit, I use one of these." From his vest pocket he withdrew a small fold of paper. He shook broken bits of a licorice into his palm, offering them first to Cowboy then selecting a big piece for himself. "Soothes the nerves."

Cowboy took the candy, but pocketed it for later on. He climbed onto the buckboard, motioning for Cal to join him. "What brings you to Cowtown?" he asked Cal. "You're not quite a *Cheechawko*, but I expect you ain't been here long."

"If by that you mean newcomer, then yes. I'm here in support of the family business. We're building a feed lot off the new railroad spur just this side of Leesville." He pointed with an extended arm to a spot true north.

"That land must have cost you dear, if'n you bought it off the railroad. Those boys ain't cheap," Cowboy said.

"And you'd be exactly right, except my grandfather owned a substantial interest in the Michigan Central line until recently Vanderbilt bought him out. The spur and the land was part of that deal," Cal said without sounding the braggart. "And before you ask, my father, along with McCormick and Lawry, ran the stockyard owned by grandfather's railroad in Chicago. He's in Nebraska now establishing a similar but larger operation. So I get this outpost as a chance to prove myself, which is great because I love this country."

Cowboy assessed the man again with this news in mind. Although young, he appeared confident if not also capable. And he sure-fire didn't panic when the little pony spooked on him. "Ain't seen it yet, but sounds like you got your work cut out," he said.

"Oh my yes," Cal blurt out with a laugh. "I have four flat cars stacked with newly milled lumber and posts from northern Minnesota just sitting on my rail siding to be unloaded. The surveyor and his people are busy from sun up to sundown staking the land out for the livestock pens. And, the labor foreman I hired three months ago in Calumet showed up two weeks late." Cal laughed a bit longer this time. "He's only now putting together a local crew." Cal's look darkened. "I only came here today looking for my trunk with all the business papers and books I've needed since the beginning. It was onboard with me when I left Chicago, but got offloaded in St. Louis somehow. They're having a devil of a time getting it the rest of the way."

"Some fellers couldn't track a steer through a bunk house," Cowboy said. "But like as not, they'll find it for you. Soon I hope." The wagon and team was just approaching the first of the mercantile buildings. Shadows were beginning to show on the sides of those structures as the sun made its way further west.

"What I really need is another set of hands," Cal said. "I need someone really good at organization and that can work well with numbers. They should like handling lots of detail and be used to dealing with strong personalities. They ought to be from around here and know the local ways." He turned to Cowboy with a half-serious look. "Above all, they need to maintain a pleasant demeanor always. Especially with me."

"Guess they'll need to turn up the wick, too, when time comes." They both laughed.

"Yes," Cal said. "That goes without saying." He seemed baffled. "I've talked with several possible folks, but found them all lacking. I doubt some could tell a housecat from a skunk." His face lightened. "It's a good position, though. They could grow with the corporation, become indispensable."

Cowboy continued to listen, but began to search the wooden walkways with his eyes.

"I suppose that I've just described some personage living on the likes of Mount Olympus or in the halls of Valhalla." Cal said. "Nevertheless, you seem like a man would who'd be a good judge of character. Anyone come to mind?"

At that moment Cowboy spotted Emma. She sat on a bench in the shade of a store's overhang. In her lap was Cowboy's hardback Bible, next to her a small pile of bags and boxes, full of the items she'd come to town for. So concentrated was she on her reading, Emma did not look up to see the wagon approach with her tall new friend and the accompanying stranger.

Cowboy swiveled on the seat to give the man his best straight-faced serious look. The slight twinkle in his eyes flashing there did not belie that effort. "Now that I think on it, Cal," he said. "I just might."

* * *

At first, Dusty only tolerated the petting and scruffing by the friendly young woman. Emma worked her hand up the long neck to the ears. Then Dusty actually leaned his shoulder towards her like some big cat pointing out a favorite place to scratch. "I think he's partial to you," Cowboy said as he heaved himself off the front porch stoop to stand next to the girl. He'd been admiring her new duds as she attended to his horse. Stout stoga boots with thick soles, ready-made canvas trousers that hung loosely on her frame, and a pullover three-buttoned shirt with its long woolen tails tucked in. A wide hat shaped into a low crown - the kind favored by wagoneers, hunters on the prairie, and Buffalo Bill Cody himself - sat atop her head.

"Cal said we'd be working outside most of the time and I'd need clothes like these," Emma offered in response to his knowing grin.

"Suits you," Cowboy admitted. He gazed back at the porch to see her few possessions stacked there: a carpet bag stuffed with clothing and a small box holding trinkets and collectibles. From that box Emma took Cowboy's leather-bound Bible. "I couldn't go without returning this." He took it with just a nod. "I read in there how important giving your word is." She said. "God kept His promise by sending His son into this world. Because of that we are all saved if we believe in Him." Cowboy smiled at both her words and the earnestness showing in her face. "Can't say as I fully understand all that I read, but I intend to keep studying it." Emma looked as happy as Cowboy had seen her. "I'll get my own Scriptures out of wages, once I pay back the advance," she said. "Spent most of that on this outfit and renting the back room at Old Miss Hagebak's house over in Leesville."

"Needn't bother," Cowboy told her. He opened the saddlebag on Dusty's hip. From that he took a small parcel wrapped in butcher paper and twine. Emma opened it, surprised to see it was a new Bible. "Last time in town, I came across the Salvation Army man down on the main street. For a few coins tossed on his drum, he was glad to part with it. He had a passel of 'em. Guess he figures Cowtown is full of sinners."

Emma blurted, "Oh, thank you." And before Cowboy could prepare himself, she jumped in with unexpected speed to throw her arms tight around his waist, burying her face in his chest. He could feel the strength of her bear hug. If not a bear, then at least a grateful cub.

"Don't get to fussin' now," Cowboy said in words barely audible. He could feel the redness flash his cheek and earlobes. "I ain't done nothing special."

Releasing her grip only with sheer reluctance, Emma studied the big man. "Oh no?" she said. "In less than the matter of one week you've managed to set right all the promises broken to me in three years. That's more than nothing."

"Did that how, exactly?" he asked.

Ticking them off with her fingers, Emma recounted, "First, my time of service at this house is finally over. Lydia found another girl to do the cleaning and such. And they're actually paying her a little something." She touched her second finger. "A complete stranger has treated me with the dignity and caring one shows to his close family. I never felt that before." She touched the last finger. "Because of you, a young man is coming this morning with his buggy. When he leaves here, he'll be taking me with him to another town." Cowboy followed her outstretched hand to where she pointed. He turned to see Cal headed toward them, pulled by a magnificent bay mare.

"I'm leaving too," Cowboy said. "Got the wood stacked and the chores done. Now's time for me and Dusty to be setting out. Got to see if I can find this other pard from my buckaroo days. Should be on the way to where I'm heading."

"Give me a promise of your own making," she asked at last. "Say that you will come see me again, when your travels are through."

Cowboy took his hat off. "I give my word," he said solemnly. Then he smiled. "It's no secret. Only way back to Texas is along that trail," He pointed. "And through this town. I'll be back." Then he grinned enough to show teeth. "I expect that by the time me and Dusty come through, you'll be Cal's *querida*."

"What's that?" she asked matching his merriment.

"South of the river it's how we call a gal our sweetheart. He's a good man, I'll let y'all work that out." Cowboy turned to mount his ride, but Emma pulled him back by the elbow. Standing on tiptoes she kissed his cheek. Tears welled in her eyes. Cowboy's too. "Adios, *chica*," he told her in farewell.

With a handshake and a word of best wishes to Cal as he stepped from the buggy, Cowboy took the saddle. They made the short distance to the trail, turning north. "She's in good hands, Dusty," the big man said. He urged the buckskin to a trot.

Cowboy and Dusty loped the trail together at an easy pace.

Their journey had begun.

A Word Given
Study Questions

1. Emma had been betrayed by people over the years, making it hard to trust what anyone said. Have you been hurt by betrayal before? What did you do about those situations? Do you have anyone in your life you can trust now? Why or why not?

2. In the Bible, Emma read about how God kept his promises. At the very beginning, he promised to send a Rescuer to fix the brokenness sin brought into the world. How does God sending Jesus show he keeps his promises? What other promises does God make in the Bible?

3. Even though God always keeps his promises, some people feel betrayed by God when their life doesn't go like they want it to. Have you felt this way? Why or why not? How does the truth of the Bible address the wrong thinking that makes people feel that way?

4. Jesus promises to return and finish the work he began. How does the promise that Jesus will come back again and make everything right address the problems you face right now? Are you willing to trust God to keep that future promise and rescue you and the world? Why or why not?

Talking Rock

The west can hide a man. For bandits on the dodge or some puncher just looking to get lonesome, open land begets miles and miles of solitude.

Cowboy's pal, Frankie Peppers, had no price on his head - this time. There was no reward poster calling for his arrest or capture, and no one had put a bounty on him either - not even under his real name. When old Uncle Chacho determined it was no lawman he was talking to, the man let slip where Peppers might be hiding out.

It took Cowboy three days riding Dusty hard, forty miles over rough ground to find where Frankie had last been spotted. A week more and he rode up to an isolated trading post to find Frankie deep in the building's shadow, sitting on a broken Montgomery Ward box. Cowboy's friend held thin rolling paper in one small hand. He shook tobacco shreds loose from a Bull Durham pouch with the other. Frankie took his time thoughtfully constructing his next precious smoke.

Cowboy could not see Frankie's eyes beneath his very wide vaquero's *chapulla* he wore flat atop his head, but there was no mistaking that familiar pointy chin. The straw hat, with its knotted rope for a hatband, came from south of the border. It was what the people there called the "shade-maker."

Striking a match against the wall, the little man drew in a lungful of breath. He tilted his head back as he did so, stopping when his eyes looked into those of the tall rider seated atop the beautiful buckskin. "Dang it, but you ain't Frankie Peppers," Cowboy said in disgust. "You sure as blazes got to be close of kin."

It took the balance of the afternoon, and the gentle inducement of hot tortillas, spicy carne, and beans cooked by the little *mamacita* in the back of the store, to get Frankie's half-brother to open up. But once fed, the man proved to be quite the talker. "Goes on just like Frankie did", Cowboy laughed to himself.

The man finally shoved the empty plate away from him, wiping his mouth on the back of a sleeve. "Ain't hiding," he said. "Not now. The fuss last summer over that man's cattle amounted to all but nothing. Sheriff didn't like it much, but he had to let Frankie go. None of them cows had any brand on 'em at all." The brother took his time poking between two back teeth with the nail of a little finger. Inspecting it, he seemed genuinely disappointed to find nothing further to eat. "This time of year Frankie and some other *vaquero* ride out to the flatlands on the other side of that mesa." He nodded at the small window in the wall beside them. Cowboy turned to see a long escarpment in the distance, blood red in color as the sun's rays struck there. He judged it to be most of a good day's ride, if not more.

"Can you say more precise the place I'd find him?" Cowboy asked.

In response the man stood. "Well," he said. Searching the store, he walked to the cook stove to select a piece of burnt remnant from the ash pile. On the way back, he took up a gray scrap of muslin he found on the floor. "You follow the creek out yonder - don't know the real name. 'Round here we call it the Salakoa - 'till you get to the river, then head west." He began to draw a map on the cloth with the thin sliver of charcoal. "There's a shallows about halfway along the mesa, an easy place to cross. Doubt the water will even come up to your stirrups this late in the season." He looked up from his crude cartography, concerned with the detail but satisfied. "Even a fiddle-foot could track the path of broken sage and chaparral Frankie made getting to the tall grass. He's not trying to hide nothing, just looking for horses. Sells them to the Army." The man handed Cowboy the drawing. He judged the big stranger could get there from where he sat, but he was careful not to ask why he seemed so determined to go.

* * *

Cowboy dipped the canteen back into the narrow stream until the bubbles disappeared. He squatted. His backside pressed against the incline of one creek bank, a leg outstretched. His boot mashed against rocks on the opposite slope. The water meandered into a shallow curve just beyond him. It turned away from the mesa without a river in sight. Should he follow the creek or head toward where he thought the tallgrass actually was?

Before he could puzzle that out, Cowboy needed to let Dusty drink too. It might be some time before they came to sweet water again. He didn't know this land, and he was about to ride away from the only true source of it he could see. Taking off his broad hat, weathered but still rain tight, Cowboy flipped it downside up. With both hands he scooped it into the stream until it filled. Then using all the skill of a P.T. Barnum circus acrobat, he whirled his belly against the steep bank and rested elbows on the level ground. Dusty drank all that was offered from this hatful, and another, and most of the third.

Cowboy clambered up next to his horse, waving the hat back and forth beside his knee to air it out as he considered their state of affairs. "You know, Dusty, at a time like this Ma would snatch me up by the shirt collar and stare into my eyes. She'd fuss I was lost as an Easter Egg." He laughed as he strapped the canteen back to the saddle. "*Estas perdido.* That's never a good thing." Cowboy looked back the way they had come. He could no longer see the timbers of the trading post roof. "Way I figure it," he said to the back of Dusty's twitching ears. "We ain't lost exactly. We're just riding lands we never crossed before."

Cowboy used the remaining sunlight and half the next day's to bring him to the mouth of the bench at the bottom of the mesa. From where he reined Dusty in, he could spot the grassland in the distance. Before that lay a maze of short canyons; most with sheer walls. For a long moment Cowboy considered the various passageways, until he selected one he judged afforded the most direct path.

Entering that first canyon, Cowboy craned his neck to gaze up the steep sides. Both were red as autumn sunset. Light refracted off quartz and feldspar scattered along seams and ledges. The air carried the whiff of something Cowboy could not ignore, but did not recognize. He did, however, detect two sets of horse prints in the loose sediment of the trail winding crookedly before him. They looked no more than a week old. "Frankie," he said, guessing; glad that none were yet returning in his direction. With the sun no longer straight overhead and hidden by high walls, Cowboy and Dusty rode in the bright diffusion of alpenglow, comfortably passing through the unfamiliar, yet enchanting, landscape.

Cowboy eased Dusty around a dog leg's bend toward the west. He expected to find the canyon widen into its exit there. Instead, he found himself staring across a small alluvial flat, an almost perfect circle some fifty feet edge-to-edge. A mass of monolithic sandstone loomed upward, to a great height, at one side of this clearing. The now unobstructed sun flooded the wall with radiant light. Cowboy sat motionless staring at what he saw twenty yards in front of him. Wonderment gripped his features.

He stepped down from Dusty with practiced ease, and led the horse by the reins to the middle of this formation. Close to the wall, a series of log-sized volcanic tuffs shaped into slags lay where they'd fallen from the mesa top. Cowboy stared up to fully examine the wall's uneven surface. It shocked him indeed that what he'd seen at a distance could be the same as he was looking at now. It was not the mirage he'd first imagined.

Ancient peoples inhabiting this region in past times obviously had selected this one spot as a holy place, Cowboy reasoned. He'd heard such campfire talk and rumor, but this was the first he'd come upon.

The bright patina of the red coloring carried a consistent hue the length and breadth of the wall. Along its surface, in groups and arcs and clusters, sizable figures appeared. Austere stick men stood next to wild animals. Concentric symbols surrounded unidentifiable markings. And, a series of arrows pointed a jagged pathway through the entire menagerie. Each appeared in bright relief to the wall's otherwise burnished color.

Cowboy slid off a rawhide glove, reaching over his head to touch the outline of the closest figure. His fingertips ran along the figure's edge for a ways, then along the rough red wall surface, and back to the figure once more. It became obvious to him that the men, animals, and symbols had not been painted on the rock as he first believed – but had, in fact, been scratched into the wall with some crude implement. The artistic gouging, he reasoned, had revealed the somewhat orangey-yellow layer underneath. How a rock could come to have two colors, Cowboy could not fathom.

While he struggled with this bafflement, he heard Dusty blow a double snort through wide nostrils followed by the beginnings of a whiny deep in the throat. It muffled out almost inaudible. Cowboy knew these to be the sounds Dusty made only when the big horse grew uncomfortable. And, that horse feared little.

Cowboy flinched, more amazed than startled to see two Arapahoe standing not six feet from him, each eyeing him with silent caution. Except for Dusty's warning, he'd not heard their approach. The old man looked at the same time both brittle and resilient. His thin frame could not be hidden by the billowing hand woven shirt. White hair covered his ears before draping over the shoulder. Thin leather gathered the locks together to resemble a pony's tail.

The other seemed no more than a child of three or four. His dark hair was matched by the even blacker eyes. He carefully kept the elder between himself and the tall stranger.

"*Tay kosh kutay?*" the old man asked in a series of guttural rumbles. He jabbed the index and middle finger of one hand in front of him, first at Cowboy then the wall. When he got no firm answer, he asked again. "*Tay kosh kutay enwende?*"

Cowboy raised both palms upward, shaking his head and giving a slight shrug of the shoulder. "I don't speak your tongue, grandfather. *Habla español?*" Neither language drew a response from the old man beyond a patient stare.

The man studied Cowboy with an unguarded curiosity that bordered on scrutiny. He saw the wrangler's knife at his hip, but noted also that no pistol hung there. After another moment's silence, he nodded once to Cowboy and turned away. The old man and boy walked without a sound to a knee-high slag that faced the sandstone. Taking up a cross-legged position on the rock, the old man raised his eyes to the sky. He began to recite a lengthy litany that continued as his eyes then affixed the wall in a blank stare.

Without warning, the man sprang to his feet and took a position close to the markings. He focused first on a thin line that curved into an almost complete loop before encircling itself again and again like some never ending whirlpool. He moved quickly next to a fantastical shaped human figure, much larger than any of the many stickmen that dotted the wall. These he pointed to as they clustered closely at one spot, only to diverge into scattered bands headed toward various compass points. For long minutes, in his deep foreign tongue, the old man called out words that to Cowboy, seemed to describe these various peoples. A flurry of pointed arrows, broken lances, and upside-down men and horses dominated the center of the wall, which brought a somber tone to the man's recitation. But as he stood just beneath the small figure of what looked like a big horn sheep pierced by three arrows, he touched this figure with his finger tips and began to wail without control. In the silence that followed, the old man stepped over to the series of intricate geometric shapes at the wall's end. He began to chant once more, one hand on the wall, the other touching just above his temple.

At last he sat next to the boy once more. Long minutes of silence followed. At intervals he would turn to the boy, whispering or speaking in low tones, he would impart some private information to the youngster.

A smile came to Cowboy's lips. "You don't need bother with them hushed tones," he said to himself more than to the Arapahoe. "I don't *sabe* any of it." He'd found his own slag to sit upon, near where Dusty fed on what sparse vegetation the horse could find thereabouts.

One hour became two as Cowboy watched the Arapahoe. Both sat without word or much movement. The old man, eyes closed, appeared in a trance. At regular intervals his head would nod a half-inch as though he were either agreeing with himself or counting off some unseen list in his head. The boy, for his part, alternated his attention between his grandfather, the wall, and the ground in front of him. It amazed Cowboy that a child so young could remain so still. Most he'd seen that age spent all their time in rambunctiousness or unfettered caterwauling.

It amazed Cowboy further that this wall captivated him so. The etchings touched a certain curiosity at the back of his mind and began plaintive stirrings in his heart. What he did not understand but could only feel, was a tug at the bottom of his soul. He confided as much to the buckskin, "It's like I've hidden something deep down inside, Dusty. A long time ago. But now I'm hankering to know the answer to questions I can't even put into words yet. It's a bafflement." The big horse bobbed his head as though he understood.

Cowboy studied the wall's figures and symbols once more. He made no further understanding as to what it all meant, but he could reckon this collection held some great message. Obviously, it did for the two Arapahoe.

His thoughts were interrupted by the sound of a horse's footfalls coming his way. Frankie Peppers stopped the pony near Cowboy's mount and slid himself quietly to the ground. He slapped Dusty on the rump and smiled.

"I thought that was you, *mi hermano*. No one rides a horse like this. Big. Sure-footed. A *Boyo Coyoté* with black stockings. Saw you through the spyglass when you came through that flat bench between the mesas. Couldn't help it. Storm clouds in the sky behind you. Made the *cayuse* stand out like blooms on prickly pear."

Cowboy smiled at his pal. He remembered how listening to Frankie's clipped staccato could wear him out. Lassoing with a stiff rope would be easier. At least the riata would get softer over time.

The little man pumped Cowboy's hand a dozen times while eyeing the old friend with some concern. "Don't see no star. You ain't law. I'm always careful who's law and who's not. No bounty hunter, I think. Too early for elk. Not enough of you to be chasing down mustangs." Frankie paused at last. "Why you here, amigo?"

Before Cowboy could answer, Frankie turned his head to stare at the two Arapahoe. He knew many of their tribe thereabouts, this close he might recognize one of them. He did.

"*Mira!*" Frankie hissed out in a slow breath.

Close-set dark eyes grew big as nickels. "White Raven himself," he whispered. "*El Borcado* of the entire Three Fires Clan. The Dream Seeker. Named him for a bird they saw the day he was born. Has the gift of vision no man - red, brown, or white - can match." Frankie turned his head back to face Cowboy. His voice still hushed in reverent tones. "The old man squats there on that Talking Rock. The one he's huddled on with the boy. Stares at this wall until his mind can see a blazing pathway. It's said he gains the power of that image. This assures the tribe's success." The little man nodded once toward the old Arapahoe, in awe. "That's big medicine."

Without waiting for Cowboy to respond, Frankie grabbed the horn of his saddle with both hands and swung himself up. "*Vamonos, amigo.* I'm not superstitious, but I don't need no hexes either." He turned his horse back the way he'd come.

Cowboy threw a leg over Dusty at the same time. Leaning hard, and with an outstretched hand, the wrangler grabbed his friend by the elbow. "Before you light out of here with that pony's tail on fire, tell me what you know about them etchings," Cowboy said. "I can figure some." He indicated the whirlpool. "And I can suppose at others." His hand swept up to the mid-wall, but stopped as he pointed. "What I want to know is why the old man cried hot tears when he put his hand on that sheep symbol. The one with all them arrows in it."

Frankie shot a hard look at Cowboy. His hurry to leave drained the color from his face. He said, "My mother's people all are Three Fires. But she took up with a Spanish *vaquero, mi padre*. We lived near the villages. I came here as a young boy to learn the stories. The people were happy once, but soon the clans took separate ways. Battles broke out between them. War to the death." Frankie was careful to look neither at the wall or White Raven, only at Cowboy. "With so much fighting, clans could not grow crops or hunt. People starved." He leaned his head back as if to better recall his teachings. "The Three Fires sent twelve young men and boys to hunt for game. Only one came back alive, carrying that big horn struck with many arrows. It was called the Dark Time." Cowboy could see the distant sadness float across his friend's face. "Meat from that big sheep kept them alive until the peace that soon followed."

Frankie spurred his horse hard, then yanked it to a stop. A thin wicked smile crossed his lips. "My father's people tell it different. The old *viejos* say Three Fires hunters," Frankie scrunched his dark face into a wrinkling of unconcealed scorn. "Not so good, eh? Very bad." He shrugged. "Why else would it take three arrows to slay one sheep? The only one they ever managed to kill, so they HAD to honor it on the wall." Frankie grinned. "Maybe old White Raven was crying for their lack of skill." He burst out

78

with a loud guffaw, showing very white and very straight teeth." It did not, however, draw the attention of either Arapahoe.

"Now that's more like the Frankie Peppers I rode the trails with," Cowboy drawled through a grin of his own. "I wondered how long you'd gab before the talk turned to food. Seems I recollect, with all we had to learn about horses and cattle, the only thing you ever wanted to know was when we'd eat."

"Maybe," Frankie said. He let the mocking grin relax into something close to impishness. "But eating's important, you know. Especially to a skinny *vatto* like me."

"I see you still can't stop a horse without jerking the reins." Cowboy said. "Surprised that apron-faced hoss didn't throw you, like some of them others did." He laughed. "How far's your camp?"

"An hour maybe," Frankie said. "If we hurry, we can get there before sundown." He tapped a saddle bag with the leather braided strap tethered to his wrist. "I got some tequila. *Poquito*, not much, but enough for tonight. We talk old times, eh?" The vaquero waited for Cowboy to ease Dusty alongside his pony. "Speaking of eating," Frankie said. "Raphael is boiling some prairie chickens and sweet grass tubers into a stew for supper. He spices them with sage bush shavings and bits of brickle weed." A pink tongue shot out to lick part of his upper lip. "*Andale, muchaco!* Time to eat!"

Before another word could be said, Frankie quirted his pony hard across the flank, jolting him into a sprint toward the mouth of the canyon. Frankie leaned forward in the saddle, almost to the nag's bobbing neck, to brace himself against the pony's lengthening stride.

Dusty needed no encouragement. In an instant, he was at full gallop hot on the pony's heels as they raced headlong toward the open prairie. Over his shoulder, Cowboy took one last glance at the wall, watching etchings disappear in a bouncing blur.

* * *

The gust from a morning wind blew ash and hot sparks from the campfire into a swirl. Cowboy and Frankie both moved where the smoke would be out of their eyes. Each held a tin of strong coffee, barely touched.

"Ray's dead? *Dios mio*," Frankie said. He made the sign of the cross quickly, kissing the back of his thumb's knuckle at the last. He glanced at the sky above him, then shook his head in disbelief. "Ray always took good care of me. Used to call me '*Franito*'. I yell at him 'I'm no thumb-sucking *niño*.' He starts calling me 'Little *Franito*' after that just to gnaw at me." Frankie pointed a thin finger at Cowboy. "He'd always buy drinks when I had no money. And, he'd finish fights I got into with those loudmouth drovers in those trail town cantinas. *Caramba*, now he's dead."

"Yessir," Cowboy smiled, recalling his friend and mentor. "The man could surely raise hell and put a chunk under it."

Frankie sat stunned in silence. Cowboy let the man have his quiet. Raphael busied himself with morning chores elsewhere, so the two had the fire to themselves.

The vaquero roused himself once more, smiling this time. "Ray always could charm the *bonitas*. The ladies loved him. And he gave me this spyglass, I don't remember why." From his range coat, Frankie pulled out a small brass telescope, once used on a Navy frigate but won by Ray with three queens and a pair of eights. Frankie stared at it now as if it were a lump of gold.

With a gloved hand, Cowboy took the pot off hot coals. He poured some in Frankie's cup, then into his own. "Ray was a good pard," he said.

"*Si*," Frankie replied. "Selling mustangs to the Army was his idea. Decent pay and more nights sleeping under the stars. Thought it would never end, but then he changed. At a campfire just like this. Not eight-ten miles north of here. Just the other side of Round Pond."

"The itinerant preacher man, that big fella?" Cowboy asked.

"Big as you, *hermano*. Maybe bigger." Frankie said. "Hands like a grizzly paw, voice louder than a cornered buffalo. Soft grey eyes that looked into yours, and knew all your secrets." He stared down at the coffee getting cold in his hand. "Said his name was Vandenaker or something like that, but just to call him Brother Van. He scared me. Ray took a shine to him. They talked all night. Next day preacher was gone. Ray was different."

"How's that?" Cowboy asked.

"We gathered up what little ponies we had and took them to the quartermaster. Got our money and headed south to Cowtown. He courted Esmerelda, went to church meetings regular, gave up drinking and fighting, and bought the boarding house with that little stable." Frankie smiled at the memory. "He married Essie and settled down to become a good citizen. His woman could sure cook, but I came back up here anyway."

"Last time I was to visit them," Cowboy said. "Ray told me his soul felt free as any mustangs galloping open prairie. He knew something I still don't know." Cowboy tossed coffee dregs on dying coals. "I came up from Texas to find just what that was, and it seems the trail has led to this Brother Van. Any idea as to his whereabouts?"

"Way he talked," Frankie said. "He liked to winter with the tribes near what those people call 'the trembling earth'. South of the Yellowstone basin." His eyes narrowed. "You think of going up there? It's a long way, amigo."

"Maybe if I knew where," Cowboy replied. "You any better at map-makin' than your kin back at the trading post?" I don't want no antigoglin path this time."

"Agh!" Frankie said. "Hildalgo's a *cabrone*." He shook his head in rapid sweeps. "You don't need no map. See that snow peak on the horizon?" He pointed to a white speck barely to be seen in the distance surrounded by deep blue sky. "Follow the water to that mountain. I hear the river starts below this rocky waterfall at one end of a high meadow. This Brother Van described his lodge squeezed along the other side." He looked at the mountain once more and counted on his fingers. "You got time to get there and back before first snows. Not by much."

"Tight," Cowboy said with more caution than certainty. "But doable. I reckon I'll chance it."

"Why ask for trouble?" Frankie asked. "There's things in the woods up there that can eat you. And the horse too." Frankie spread his palms out wide. "Does this have something to do with that look you had when I rode up in the canyon? When you were watching those two from the tribe."

"It wasn't them, it was the etchings." Cowboy said. "That was a pretty big wall. I knew what was up there had meaning, but I couldn't make sense of it. A song with verses missing." Cowboy pulled the leather bound book from his coat. "It reminded me so much of the first time I took up the Scriptures out on the trail. The more pages I read, the more muddled it became. No matter how powerful I knew the words to be." He put the book away. "I couldn't do it by myself. My brother Marcus helped me some, my father too. I was hoping Ray could give me some guidance like he always did for me on the trail."

Cowboy stood to put his tin cup back in the saddle bag. He began to adjust Dusty's cinch. In a moment more, he turned back to Frankie. "Shared a bunkhouse with this fella from England. Smart hombre, *mucho* schooling. We called him the Professor. Said something I'll never forget, so I made him write it down. "

From the inside pocket of his coat Cowboy removed a rumpled paper. "Frenchman named Pascal studied numbers. He thought a lot about a man's mind. And heart, too. He said this." Cowboy read from the script in his hand. "'There is a God shaped vacuum in the heart of every man which cannot be filled by any created thing, but only by God, the Creator, made known through Jesus.'"

He returned the paper to its hiding place. "I got that exact emptiness, Frankie," Cowboy said. I ain't a man who goes barkin' at a knot, so if it takes trekking to that mountain to help me find Jesus, so be it."

Cowboy gazed at the snow peak for a moment. He stuck out his hand for Frankie to shake. "Best of luck with the ponies, *compadre*. I'll look for you on my way home."

"I only see good things in your travels," Frankie said at last. *Viya con Dios, hermano.*"

Cowboy turned Dusty toward the worn track that ran along the river's edge.

They loped the trail together at an easy pace.

Their journey had begun.

Talking Rock
Study Questions

1. Cowboy saw the Arapahoe talk and heard about the change in Ray. It made him think about the emptiness he felt inside. Have you felt that same feeling, that emptiness inside and sense that others had something you didn't have? What did you do about it?

2. Cowboy read the quote that there is a God-shaped hole in every person's heart. Do you think this is correct? Why or why not? How do people have an emptiness in their hearts for something they have never known?

3. People use all kinds of things to try and fill the emptiness we feel inside. What kinds of things do people use to try to fill that emptiness? Can anything satisfy that emptiness? Why or why not?

4. Cowboy couldn't decipher the drawings on the wall. Do spiritual things feel like the ancient drawings that Cowboy found—things you just can't decipher? How should you go about figuring out what they mean?

Somedays

"Beauty can fool any man, even if he's mindful."

Cowboy heard his father's words rumble through his head again as plainly as if the old man were standing right beside him. "Sweet smells tempt him," the parson droned on. "But unexpected touches of the hand surely make his heart go giddy-up. And, whispered promises cloud the otherwise most even judgment." He thumped the Good Book in front of him, concluding: "There's danger when distraction addles a mind away from steadfast thinking."

Riding through the lodge pole pines, Cowboy recalled that confusing lecture, or whatever it was, when the Gospel Man gathered his boys in their tiny Atascosa kitchen. His father truly believed the day drew near when their bubbling adolescence might compromise proper treatment of those few females close of age living thereabouts.

No concern for the fairer sex back home made Cowboy reminisce that awkward evening. Instead the thought came triggered by Frankie's warning, not one week past, about those things living in the woods through which he now traveled.

Cowboy could not help but marvel at what he saw, and smelled, about him. Across the plains of Texas where he'd wrangled cattle years on end, a tree'd be thought "tall" if it grew as high as Dusty's ears. This army of evergreens he gazed at stretched overhead more than ten times his own height. Each tree spanned the width of a broad man's shoulders. Its leaves like substantial mending needles, but emerald green in hue.

Cowboy drew a needed deep breath in this thinning air. The strong scent permeating the thicket carried a heady tang to Cowboy's nostrils. It brought sweet metallic taste to his tongue.

Giving himself a hard shake in the saddle, Cowboy threw off the dreamy daze that had begun to grab hold of him. This brought him back to his usual keen awareness. In caution, he slid the rifle halfway out the scabbard and back in again, wanting the Remington ready should he need it at the haste.

The act of touching that weapon reminded Cowboy that should he not find Brother Van in the next day or so, he'd need to stalk some game for food. Or, he'd be reduced to eating *pinyon* nuts from the many pinecones strewn along the way. He might even have to chance trapping one of those red-backed Chicaree – what the folks out this way call their chattering shade-tail squirrels.

"Sun's full up," Cowboy told Dusty. "But don't seem to make it to ground betwixt these tall trees. Breeze become a wind now, and makes the air a might coolish this high up the mountain." He rolled the range coat's collar tight against his neck, wrapping his bandana round it just to keep the chill off his skin.

Reining Dusty to a stop, Cowboy pondered their changing situation. The trail they'd ridden ended, edging a wide-spread deep ravine. The slope bottomed at a gushing, fast-moving stream. That, in turn, emptied into the river the two had followed since the mesa. Scattered boulders clinging to both embankments evidenced sizeable rock slides in the region, but none recent.

For a moment, Cowboy chewed on the notion that it would be next door to a miracle just to ride Dusty safely down this incline, let alone cross that flood. Even if he managed that he figured, they'd need a stroke of luck to heave themselves up the steep bank on the opposite side. "A risk not worth taking," he nodded to himself. Another go-across somewhere upstream would need the finding. Just the same, he took the time to stare through trees beyond this noisy gorge, seeing piney woods give way to an undersized but sunlit clearing. Cowboy reckoned this likely not the preacher's meadow, but it might be holding an elk or two.

Hopeful then about the prospect of fresh backstrap and tenderloins for supper, Cowboy turned his horse away from the river. He nudged the buckskin into a slow walk, letting Dusty pick his way, sure-footed, among the many rocks now scattered on the meager path. For long minutes Cowboy rode chest bent to saddle horn, studying the dirt in the path that ran nearly parallel to the creek. Others had passed this way ahead them. Some weeks before, judging by the impressions he saw. The hoof prints there in the mud came from a barefooted pony, and not one Indian-shod either. Various animal tracks mixed in with them as well. That made the first sign he'd seen of another rider since he left the tallgrass flatlands. It could be a mountain man, or perhaps the preacher himself. Cowboy hoped it might portend well.

Topping the rise, Cowboy could see the water below him actually jetted through a rock-strewn hollow in the hillside some quarter-mile up the way. This formed a natural span above the stream. It seemed the traveler's path would cross there too.

Along the track in front of him lay several outcroppings of weathered granite. Each extended out far enough to force the trail around it on its way toward the arching bridge. It amazed Cowboy that these craggy formations evidenced so much tremendous upheaval. Great slabs of rock leaned hard against adjacent slabs of rock. Occasionally, narrow gaps occurred between, none wider than could barely hold a man. Dens perhaps, for the smallest of wildlife.

Cold wind gusts coming from the river freshened at Cowboy's back. This caused unruly hair to flail against his cheeks and brow. He tugged his big hat further down and guided Dusty around that first tall ledge.

Squinting now at that stretch between them and the bridge, Cowboy realized that Frankie's premonition had come to pass.

* * *

Standing flat on two hind paws, a bear fattened by a summer full of eating leaned forward to grab a slender tree trunk in its sizeable claws. He held the grip just about at chin level. His big head canted all the way sideways right. With its mouth now full open, the bear managed to get its jaws around the entire tree. Slobbering, it scraped the bark back and forth with long incisors.

This left both markings and scent for all creatures coming along this path to find, especially any other bears that might also occupy this stretch of mountain.

The bear froze in place. For a moment, no sound could be heard except the air sucked in and panted out of its protruding nose. It had caught the scent of something new. Abandoning the tree, it stood erect. The head jerked over a rounded shoulder in the direction of that smell. The bear's dark eyes narrowed on the sight of horse and rider. It seemed to consider whether these two were predator or prey.

Dusty saw the creature a split-second before Cowboy did. They did not react to it the same. The wrangler lurched over to grab his weapon at that same moment when Dusty staggered a violent half-step sideways, beginning the turnabout back the way they'd come. This jumble of confused movements landed Cowboy hard on the ground with a thump. His horse – and the still sheathed rifle – now raced away at the full gallop.

That left just Cowboy and the bear. The cowman knew defending himself against this considerable beast with only the knife on his belt would be the sheer act of a fool. For once, he followed his Ma's often repeated advice. He walked away from a fight. For about two steps, then he ran.

The bear, for his part, thundered out a terrifying bellow that Cowboy wagered could be heard in the next valley over. The animal dropped to all fours, head swaying side-to-side. For one guarded moment, it watched Dusty run off in a noisy clip-clop. It took another quick sniff at the wind. Then this corpulent predator concentrated its complete attention on Cowboy; smaller, slower, and fumbling now in a panicked retreat. In an explosion of speed not seemingly possible by a creature of its unwieldy size, the bear tore after the fleeing human.

Cowboy knew from campfire talk that a bear could match the fastest pony in a foot race, even up to a country mile. He stood no chance at running. The rock formation afforded his only possible hope. Grasping a handhold just over his head, Cowboy tried to pull himself up to begin an uncertain climb, but his boots could get no firm purchase on the flat granite surface.

He didn't need to turn to know how close the bear was getting. Cowboy could hear the breathy grunt expelled each time that hairy monster's front paws landed. The bear sprang off again almost at once. By then, the hind paws had caught up in this series of quickening running leaps. With the beast now almost on him, Cowboy abandoned the second attempt to climb the ledge at that spot. He scurried toward another where the rocks looked more likely to give him his ascent. He did not get there.

Unexpected, but providentially provided, the big man slid sideways into a narrow crevice between two rock slabs. Although not wide, the cleft extended from the muddy ground where Cowboy stood to the outcropping's uneven crest. The gap narrowed as it reached upward but never fully closed out the dimming sunlight. Its cramped opening could not accommodate the width of Cowboy's weathered Stetson. The hat scraped off and fell to the base of the opening. No sooner than his John B. hit the ground, a big paw swatted it away.

The protective cranny provided scant space to accommodate the big man. With the back of his head rubbing the granite behind him, Cowboy could turn his head almost without his nose touching the rock wall in front of him. His range coat and vest added enough extra bulk that Cowboy could feel the walls press his chest and back. And although the cleft ran six to seven feet deep, a flat rock's protrusion stopped Cowboy about halfway back. Catching him just at the hip, this rock, the size of a dinner plate, looked no thicker than his little finger. It did not, however, budge when Cowboy pressed a palm down on it using all his strength. He needed to squeeze back further, away from the opening, before the bear figured out that it could likely reach Cowboy with a long foreleg extended.

The snout came in first, poking barely into the opening. The bear sniffed a bit, clacking teeth together as it did so. Cowboy then watched with great revulsion as the jaws jacked open again. The bear let go an unnatural sound, less a roar and more a screech of pain. It unnerved the wrangler that he heard it to be the cry of frustration. Cowboy knew it signaled the great beast's obsession to snag him, no matter how long or what effort it eventually took. The cave filled with the stench carried by the bear's breath. That reeked of carrion and rotted gooseberries. Cowboy had never smelled the like.

Next, the big head turned sideways so that one angry eye glared at the human. Cowboy found it fitting the ear he could now see was missing a chunk of the top half. The jagged remains indicated a bite mark. The bear took time to look up and down both walls of the cleft. It stared at the topside opening for a long moment as well. Cowboy guessed the bear was searching for some other way in. Tentatively, it pawed hard at each side of the opening, but nothing gave way.

Cowboy's breathing came faster now. His attempts to break the rock plate continued to fail. Even though he knew it was coming, he still jerked when the bear whirled around to scrunch his shoulder into the breach. A searching paw, flailing claws extended, thrust at his knee caps. One large claw swiped across the toe of the boot. That left two deep scratches. That claw, blunted from continuous digging in the dirt and ripping at tree bark, split almost a third of the way up. A second swipe caught the hem of Cowboy's jeans. That removed a small tattering of cloth.

Cowboy leaned as far back as he could. He managed to avoid the next few swipes, so the bear withdrew that paw. In its place, the animal maneuvered to switch legs. In that few seconds lull, Cowboy whispered a prayer. "Lord, please help me," he said. "Don't let it end like this. I come a long way to find answers from that preacher man." The second paw probed the crevice with movements more awkward than the first. "I can't do this by myself," Cowboy went on. "I see now that I never could."

In this new posture, the bear seemed not to be able to reach in as far. Claws barely, but clearly, missed the boot with each swipe. So again, the animal readjusted, going back the original and more successful position with the other foreleg.

Cowboy felt his breathing relax. A cautious stillness seeped into his consciousness. Using just the heel of his palm at the exposed end of the protruding rock plate, he lifted up on tiptoes to bring his full weight and muscle to bore down on it. Long seconds he strained against it, ignoring the bear completely. First a muffled cracking sound, then a loud snap as the rock tumbled to the ground. In two-and-a-half sidesteps Cowboy was to the back of the crevice, out of the bear's reach. Looking at the broken rock at his feet with unbelieving eyes, Cowboy said, "This grateful sinner thanks You for that, Lord, with a humble heart." He eased out a long sigh. To restore himself further, Cowboy let his body go limp against the wall, his cheekbone pressing flat against the rock. "I won't let Your act of kindness, to help me here, go to waste."

* * *

The remainder of the morning blurred into a series of swiping paws, threatening growls, clacking teeth, snorts, sniffs, and hateful looks as the bear continued to hound his cornered prey. Cowboy wondered how long the bear's resolve would last, and what he himself would do exactly once the predator was gone.

Cowboy didn't have to wonder long. With his head looking away from the opening, it took him a moment to realize that all noise had stopped. He turned to see the entrance unencumbered of fearsome beast. Figuring it some trick to draw him into the open, the wrangler stayed right where he stood but strained to hear all sounds for some foretelling clue.

Without the animal blocking his view now, Cowboy could look out and see a tiny part of the meadow and most of the bridge that crossed the rushing stream. Two hours passed. In the distance, through that narrow opening, Cowboy watched a bear amble across the crest of the span. It made its way to the meadow, rolls of fat rippling with every step. Even that far away, Cowboy could see the gotched-ear. His tormentor had moved on.

Standing so long in such a crooked position left Cowboy somewhat stiff. Stretching helped, but what the cowman really wanted was the comfort of finding Dusty. He curled lower lip against teeth, sticking his tongue behind and let out a whistle. Loud, long, high-pitched, and shrill. He waited, but nothing. Cowboy turned to watch the bear one last time. He saw the brute turn east at entering the meadow, away from the trail.

Again he whistled, and this time in the distance Cowboy heard Dusty's muted whinny. The third whistle brought the big horse trotting up to Cowboy's side.

91

"It's good to see you, you old hoss." He said to himself as much as the horse. For a long moment he petted Dusty. That seemed to reassure the animal a bit, but gave him greater comfort. At the same time, Cowboy checked the horse for signs wounds or injury. That whole while he stood where he could still keep an eye on the bridge and the meadow, and all that space in between.

Grabbing the reins, Cowboy swung up into the saddle he thought he'd never ride again. As he considered the wisdom of pushing up the trail knowing the bear had gone nearly that same way, his thoughts were interrupted by the sounds of a tremendous commotion. Coming from a spot in the meadow blocked by the tree line and in the direction where the bear had turned, a familiar roar echoed across the gorge. It came in waves, one of anger, one of ferocity, each growing in intensity.

Cowboy suspected that the bear finally found the prey he hungered for, but that unlike him, this one put up something of a fight. Before long all the clamor stopped and the mid-mountain peace returned.

He gave the brute time enough to gorge himself. Cowboy figured a well-fed bear was a slow-moving bear. He planned to cling to the trees at the meadow's edge, skirting in the opposite direction along the trail. He pulled the rifle from its sheath, nonetheless, to hold as he rode. He would not be empty-handed again if he faced that bear a second time.

With this plan in mind, Cowboy rode Dusty across the bridge and into the clearing. At first, he did not believe what he saw there. Stopping at a distance, seeing no movement, Cowboy eased Dusty closer. The horse did not spook on him this time. Dusty sensed no danger in that big heap lying there in the meadow grass.

Cowboy stepped down. Rifle in hand, he moved to the carcass. *"What in tarnation?"* he said, still not believing. At his feet the gotched-eared bear lay dead.

"Doggone, that's not the fate I woulda expect of you. And sure as blazes not today." Cowboy scanned the space between every tree that edged the meadow. Anything that could have done this would be an even bigger monster. A greater threat to him and Dusty, but Cowboy saw nothing of the like. Only the competing sounds of jays and chattering squirrels could be heard filling the grassy clearing.

He squat on his boots to take a closer look at the bloody dead body of the beast that had tormented him so. It lay twisted on its belly; one shoulder to the ground, the other jacked at an odd angle towards the sky. The skull looked brutally crushed. One eye clung to the socket only by a small flap of skin. Twin puncture wounds, six inches apart, perforated the snout in several places.

Cowboy touched the broken head. He considered for a moment the massive force needed to inflict this much damage. He could understand the shredded throat and the scratches on the neck. What he could not fathom was the huge chunk of flesh missing from the dead bear's rump. About twice the size of Cowboy's fists balled together, tooth marks showed this hunk of meat had been bitten off. "Dang," he said. "That's plain mean."

A quick scan of the trees again, and Cowboy shoved the rifle back in the leather sheath. He turned back to the bear one last time. "If I was to ponder all this out," he told the heap of fur and bones. "I'd say we both got schooled some today. And it was all about arrogance." He looked down to see the claw with the long split pressed partly in the soft ground. "You thought you was the meanest thing in the valley. Carried on always surly and disagreeable, like some bushwacker raised on sour milk. Then you met the one that done you in. Another more vicious than you."

Cowboy touched the split claw with his finger, feeling the roughness of its surface. "My own self? My arrogance grew from all that I learned as a cowman, the skills I developed, and the trust I have – or had – in myself. A day in the cave took all that out of me." He poked now at the ribs and spine with the heel of his hand. "Ray once told me, 'It's not so much over-estimating yourself that'll get you in trouble. It's underestimating the other things around you.' Your failing was to pick on the wrong opponent. Shoulda run. Mine was to think I was boss in charge, and not admitting God is running the outfit."

Cowboy stood. "My brother Marcus often reminds me that Scripture foretells God will humble the proud and vanquish the ruthless." He studied the cut on his boot. "Today I know that to be true."

Cowboy mounted Dusty, thought better of it, then climbed back down. A grave look clouded the wrangler's eyes. "Some days," was all he said. He tried, but failed, to put a weak smile on his lips. "Some days a fella's more grateful than glad." Cowboy reached inside the coat to draw the knife from his belt. An hour later Cowboy took the saddle again, leading Dusty to the far side of the meadow.

They loped the trail together at an easy pace.

Their journey had begun.

Somedays
Study Questions

1. When Cowboy was facing the bear, he prayed a simple prayer. Was this the right approach when facing a crisis? Why or why not?

2. The encounter with the bear caused Cowboy to think about how his life could be over far more quickly than he imagined. How do encounters like that help us realize that we are not in control of our lives? Why do we think we ever are in control of our life? Are you trusting your own abilities? Why or why not?

3. Cowboy compared the bear's pride in thinking he could get Cowboy with Cowboy's own pride. Why did Cowboy see a connection between the bear's choice to go after him and his own failing to admit that God is in charge? Do you think you control your own life or that God does? What can you change to remember that God is the ruler in your life?

4. After the ordeal is over, Cowboy says that some days he just has to be grateful. Are you grateful for what you encounter on hard days? Why or why not? Is gratefulness the right response when things are hard? Why do you think that?

Bison's Dilemma

"I come a long way to find this man, Dusty. I just never expected to find him nekkid." He laughed those words out as he looked down between the horse's ears from that small bluff overlooking the waterfall.

Cowboy shuddered at the sight. Not from seeing the pale wet skin, but the knowing that the high mountain river Brother Van bathed in flowed ice-cold. A surprisingly-wide, cascading torrent crashed the rocks below with unabated roar. This formed a large catch pool, filled with swirls and eddies. Narrowing, it became the river once again. Somewhat of a light rolling mist clung to the water's surface. "Ain't exactly headwaters," Cowboy said to his mount. "But might as well be. It's as far as we're going."

He eased the big horse down a winding path, around the last of a thick pine grove, and into the open. The meadow appeared even bigger than Cowboy remembered Frankie's sketchy depiction being. His saddle pal got most of the detail right. The waterfall verged the west end of this huge high-mountain pasture, and a small cabin snugged the hillside at the tree line to the east. It took Cowboy all of several minutes to trot Dusty the distance to the riverbank.

As the wrangler approached this solitary figure, the man shook more water from his bushy hair and continued buttoning his faded union suit. Frankie's description came fairly close; the girth and height was nearly that of Cowboy. The man watched the horse and rider with an open expression, unguarded eyes, and a passive smile. At no time in Cowboy's approach did the man show any unease, much less alarm.

"Howdy," Cowboy said as he reined Dusty to a stop. "Ain't you a mite chilly standing there in just your long johns? I reckon that water's got to be more than a tad coolish this time of year."

"Truly," the man said. "The Yassahanna is not known for its warmth." He gazed at some ripples near the shore. "Instead, our river is celebrated for its great mystic quality."

"How's that?" Cowboy asked, caught up with curiosity.

The man responded with a toothy grin, "The native people say that any person that touches it can only utter the truth thereafter."

He looked up at the rider for a long moment of silence. At last he said, "Tall cowboy, riding a big buckskin with a white star on the face, broad-brimmed Stetson, and a stout mustache." He narrowed his stare, looking into the other's face. "I can't see your eyes underneath that hat of yours, but I'll wager that they're blue or grey. Tilt your head back a bit." Cowboy did so. "Indeed," the man went on. "Just what I said. A pale grey-blue. That makes you Ray Patterson's friend." The man stood motionless as he waited for Cowboy to acknowledge that obvious fact.

Astonishment flashed Cowboy's features as the wrangler struggled with the notion that he'd just ridden a thousand miles to find this stranger he hoped was Brother Van, only to hear that the man already knew him. Or at least the man knew whatever Ray had told him.

"I'm Brother Van," the man said. "I expect Ray spoke some about me, too." With a casualness borne of a peaceful confidence, he slid boots over bare feet. Next, he donned a thick woven-wool coat with very large hand-made buttons. The man walked through the ankle-high meadow grass to stand almost touching Dusty's shoulder. Raising a massive hand, he gave Cowboy's a firm shake.

"You look tuckered from your travels," Brother Van said. The preacher himself did not. His entire countenance beamed a formidable energy. "Let's head back to the cabin," he continued. "And I'll feed you a decent meal. Then I'll share with you how, intended or not, the timing of your arrival is fitting. Happenstance, I believe, but you certainly have cut it close."

Cowboy wheeled Dusty back around while Brother Van mounted his own horse, a silver-dappled dark-brown pony. Its tail and mane flowed pure flaxen. The wrangler noticed at once, as they trotted across the meadow together, the preacher's horse struck ground with a single-footed gait. It obviously was bred to handle the steeps and falls of the mountain trails.

Cowboy noticed as well that Brother Van kept eyeing the big bundle tied behind Dusty's saddle, but the man said not a word until they reached the tiny pine-log structure butted against the small hill. Once inside, Cowboy saw the cabin held more room than he would have thought. The front wall with its single door entrance and the two sides were stacked pine. But what should have been the back wall opened into a cave-like hollow that quickly tapered into the narrows of an old mine entrance.

"It gives me more space than I need, but a pleasant retreat to cool off in when the summers get too heated," Brother Van said following Cowboy's big-eyed gaze into the tunnel. "Go ahead and settle your horse while I get the fire started. I can fix us up some fresh partridge; just brought down this morning; some beans, and day-old sourdough with a little black lick to sop it in."

That brought a smile to the wrangler's face and almost a rumble to his belly as he tended to Dusty. He placed the bedroll with its tarp and soogans on the ground, and the saddle next to it, but the big bundle he lugged into the cabin. "My ma taught us to never go empty-handed whenever we come to be a guest, especially if we was to ask a favor." Cowboy said. "I thought you might could use this up here in snow country." He undid the leather thong and unrolled the furry hide with the toe of his boot. Taking the bulging muslin cloth packed in the center, Cowboy pulled back a corner to reveal the choice meat he'd cut from the dead bear's carcass after he'd skinned him just the day before. "You can add this to your skillet," he said.

Brother Van bent to take the bearskin between his fingertips. He rubbed the fur with gentle strokes, occasionally tugging at the long hairs, and finally he sniffed the skin of the underside. "This is quite fresh," he said. "Did you trade for it?" The preacher looked up at Cowboy. "Or did you kill it yourself?" He then hefted the skin in both hands over his head as high as he could stretch. Another foot-and-forty-inches and Brother Van might have lifted it all off the cabin floor. The top of the preacher's gray head almost reached that of Cowboy's. But unlike the wrangler, the man's chest barreled like a pine's trunk.

"I done neither," Cowboy replied. "Me and what was this bear spent most of the daylight yesterday, him trying to claw me out of the hole I was hiding in, me squeezin' to make myself smaller."

He raised up his right boot, pointing to the scratch. "That's him," he said. "And this is what done it." Cowboy pulled a thick, curved claw from his vest pocket. It held the deep split stretching a third of the way up from the blunted tip. Fresh saw cuts marked the jagged other end. "After a fashion, the beast got tired of coming up empty and just sauntered off," Cowboy continued. "By the time I gathered my horse back, the bear had walked over the ridge and out of sight. But when we rode up the trail to head your way, I come across his torn-up remains in this little meadow."

"A hole, you say?" Brother Van let his scruffy eyebrows furl almost together in curious disbelief.

"Yessir," Cowboy said. "He spooked my horse and I had to run for it afoot. Only the hand of God coulda led me to that narrow crevice in the rock wall. Saved me from certain dismemberment."

The preacher studied first the wrangler's boot and then his face long enough to assay the big man's worthiness. "Providential, most certainly," he said. His grave features relaxed into a smile. "Just like Moses, the Lord placed you in the cleft of the rock. A safe place for both of you, it turns out." In a voice much more bass than his generous body would indicate, the preacher burst out into loud but lovely song:

"He hideth my soul in the cleft of the rock,
That shadows a dry, thirsty land.
He hideth my life in the depths of his love,
And covers me there with his hand,
And covers me there with his hand."

A warm smile drew across Cowboy's lips. He did not know the words to that hymn, but for a moment he imagined his Pa singing this very tune. He nodded his approval. "Wish I'd known that song yesterday. I'da shouted it at that bear to leave me alone," he said. Cowboy rolled the fur back up, tying the leather lash tight once again.

"I started to ride away from his remains," Cowboy nodded at the pelt. "But got myself back off Dusty. I wanted that broken claw as a reminder." He looked almost embarrassed to continue. "'Sides, I needed meat anyway. And figured his couldn't be any tougher than some of them storm-killed longhorns we'd eat pushing the herds up north. So, I skinned him." Cowboy touched the fur with the toe of his boot. "I brought you the hide. Might need another robe, or coat, or blanket for the winters this far north." He took a step back.

Brother Van eyed the ragged hole at the bear's rump. "That done by the beast that killed him?" he asked. Cowboy dipped his head "yes." The preacher held the gotched-ear skin between thumb and forefinger, "This looks bitten off," he said. "But these cuts are fresh. Yours?" Brother Van traced a finger over a series of alternating deep grooves along the ear's gnawed edge.

"They are for a fact," Cowboy grinned. "I notched him like a newborn calf, so anyone who can read the double over-bit earmark will know this critter belongs to the Bar Diamond D. That's the brand of the family ranch back down in Atascosa County."

The preacher said nothing, only giving the taller man the beginnings of a knowing grin. "I'm just grateful something else done him in, so I didn't have to tangle with him again," Cowboy said. "My tormentor one hour, laid low in the next."

"Indeed," Brother Van said, taking in the thought. "Thank you, son. You've given me more than you know." The preacher touched the skin once more; this time with a delighted admiration. "The local native tribes place great respect on the bear, his ferocity, and great strength. That gives this pelt big enchantment. They will see it this way: You were on a pilgrimage to see me when this bear attempted to prevent your journey. But through the power of your skills, you evaded the bear and outwitted him by staying just out of reach in those rocks. You even taunted him by letting him scratch only your boot." The preacher let the story carry him to even greater rhetoric. "As punishment for his misdeed of interference, the bear was killed on your behalf by an even bigger bear. Your journey here continued without further incident." Nodding, Brother Van waved his hand in Cowboy's direction. "That makes you a man of big medicine. That all this was done so you might meet up with me, I must therefore be big medicine, too."

Brother Van patted the skin with approval while Cowboy struggled to digest what had just been explained. "That's some yarn," the wrangler said, looking from the man to the pelt and back again.

"Yes," the preacher replied. "And I intend to tell it just that way, if not more embellished, to Manatah, chief of the Bend-in-the-River peoples with whom I spend the winter months. He'll receive it with great honor and we will become even greater friends." Brother Van raised himself to full height as his faced darkened in full concentration. He waited until their eyes met. "You didn't ride all the way up this mountain merely to hand over a bearskin, even a stately one. What's really on your mind?"

A simple enough question and the one Cowboy struggled with each long day in the saddle getting to this very meadow. "I saw the change Ray made in his life. He became a better man. He found the peace that came with his devout convictions. No matter that he was so wild in his past." Cowboy's eyes stared at the preacher but his gaze turned inward. "I have wrestled with myself, been of two minds, and come up short on how to find such contentment. No matter how much I read Scripture or how many sermons that I hear delivered; or even all the feeble prayers I've tried to say — that calm escapes me." Fatigue began to sap his strength.

"Any notion as to what keeps you from finding it?" Brother Van asked. "I can't imagine that with all Ray told me of his past that you kicked up any more sand than him."

The words caused Cowboy to suck up a quick breath. He let the air back out slow. "That's the nub of it, preacher. I did do worse. I pummeled this other fellow something vicious back home in Atascosa when I was little more than a youth. Broke him up bad." Cowboy shook his head with the dreaded memories. "Then I took to the cattle drives. Thought at first it was to spare my folks the upshot of all the mess, but I've come to know that mostly I was just running away from what I had done." Cowboy sank down on the only chair in the cabin. Brother Van watched him agonize there but said nothing, waiting for him to finish in his own time. "The boy's daddy owned the bank that held papers on our ranch," Cowboy all but whispered. "I knew for sure Ma and Pa would lose that and have to take up somewhere else. All because I had a stubborn streak, quick fists, and wouldn't back down to the likes of him." Cowboy's weariness grew more pronounced the longer he confessed. "I come a long way for your help."

Brother Van sat next to Cowboy, on the cot wedged against the timbers in the wall. He stared gravely at the sight of the torment gripping this man who'd traveled so far from home to rid himself of it. "Seems like forgiveness, or more precisely the lack of it, figures into what you just told me. But know this." The preacher took the Bible, which Cowboy had slipped from his coat pocket, out of the big man's grip. "I am not the answer. You'll find that here." He held up the small leather book before handing it back. Then he placed an extended finger on Cowboy's chest. "And with prayer, you'll find it here. Because of the cross, all your sins have already been pardoned."

Cowboy looked up from staring at his boots. "Pa's a man of the Gospel, and so's my brother Marcus. I've heard and read Scripture all my life. Even on the trail." He looked at the Bible in his hand. "Since I left home, whenever I read verse about the Lord's sacrifice and the grace folks were given I know it's talking about everyone else but me. What I done is too bad." His head went back down.

The preacher's quiet laugh broke the silence. He patted Cowboy's knee until the wrangler looked up again. "From what I've heard about you from your old pal Ray, and from what I can tell from your manner in this short while, you're a man who places great store in honesty." He seized Cowboy's Bible once more. "The Lord's forgiveness for all who believe is found in numerous Gospel verse; that's the written word of the Almighty himself. He has made us His promise."

The preacher smiled a knowing smile. "I can see that you're good-sized, from boots to brisket. But I don't think that even you are big enough to call God a liar."

Cowboy sat in continued silence, pulse evident at his temples, weariness bordering on defeat in his eyes. "Can't argue with that; sure enough," he said. "But what do I do now?" he asked.

Brother Van crossed his arms as he gathered the proper words for his answer. "I spend the winters far north of here, in a place where the ground trembles and ground water boils in shallow pools. The whiff of sulfur always clings to the air." He leaned forward to put his hands on his knees. "When the snows get deep, you'll find a bison or two huddled near that gurgling water just trying to keep warm. They won't freeze to death if they stay near the pools. But the problem is, there's no food to be found there. Nothing grows close to all that ancient sulfate. To feed themselves they must venture out in chest deep snow. Some ways away they'll stop to paw that snowfall to find the grass and vegetation buried underneath." He smiled with the knowledge of what he himself had seen. "I call that the Bison's Dilemma. Stay warm and starve or chance freezing but be fed."

Cowboy followed this tale of nature with obvious fascination. He could not, however, hide his underlying puzzlement. "That's a fact about those stumpy critters I did not know." he said. "How's that figure into Scripture or my own troubled situation?"

"The way I see it," Brother Van said. "Like the bison, you have a choice to make. Stay where you are in the familiar, somewhat comfortable state of your self-imposed unforgiveness, and starve yourself spiritually. Or, you can venture from there, accept the Grace of God, and get your soul fed forever." The preacher spread his palms. "The decision is yours."

A glint of understanding began to flicker in Cowboy's eyes. He smiled.

"Let's get some supper going and follow that with a good night's rest," Brother Van said. "We both have a long day in front of us after sun up. I must leave for the tribes tomorrow if I intend to beat the first snows." The preacher's eyes revealed a growing fondness. "You found me just in time."

Cowboy still sat with elbows on knees, holding the Bible in both hands. The preacher placed both of his own atop the wrangler's. "You might want to read Acts 13:38-39 while I cook."

* * *

The morning sun had yet to peek above the ridgeline. Cowboy spent the most of two hours hustling to help Brother Van bundle the last of his portable goods and possessions from the cabin onto the pack animal's back and into the panniers. Looking at the heap of cargo lashed to the sawbucks, he reckoned the preacher subscribed to the notion, "Don't worry about the mule, load the saddle down."

"I do believe that, except for the last of the firewood and kindling, you got everything that was in there." Cowboy nodded to the tiny cabin.

"Not quite," Brother Van replied. "One last particular." He hurried off to retrieve it. In the minutes that passed, Cowboy did a quick tally of the entirety he'd seen the day before and of what he'd helped pack. He couldn't conjure up anything that they'd missed.

The preacher returned with a well-worn Big Fifty in one hand, and two stout pasteboard boxes in the other. Cowboy recognized the Sharps .50 caliber buffalo gun at once. He figured Brother Van kept it to hunt the elk on this mountain, but wondered why he kept it so hidden.

"I almost forgot that I had this," the preacher said. "I wanted you to take it." He offered up both hands to Cowboy. "Too big for my liking, but you might find it comes in handy if you face another bear on the trail going down the mountain." The man looked relieved when Cowboy took the rifle and ammunition from him.

"A man just don't give away one of his firearms like this," Cowboy insisted. "I couldn't let you go without."

"Tut-tut, young man," Brother Van said. "My .44 Henry will do me fine, and by-the-by it isn't mine. It originally belonged to a Franklin Horton. The late Mr. Horton foolishly left it leaning against a lodge pole pine thirty yards from where he scratched the rocks up near the pass looking for gold trace." The preacher shook his head at the thought. "The bear he encountered there made short work of him. Next to the Sharps, I found a lead rope tied to the tree with a halter still fastened to it; skin and hair left on the crownpiece. Apparently, the mule chose to lose a little flesh rather than suffer the same fate as Horton." The preacher's head shook again. "I didn't see that animal on that day nor have I since. I haven't heard it either. Goodness knows mules are not quiet animals, especially when they're lonely."

Cowboy agreed with a knowing nod, but looked at the rifle in his hand with some concern. Sensing that, as much as seeing it, the preacher offered, "I would not take such a weapon as this to the tribes. Even as a gift, it would only cause trouble. Before you rode up I figured that in the spring, I'd take it with me on the circuit and swap it for something at the trading post. Now I have a fine bearskin in its place."

At the mention of that word Brother Van's eyes widened in thought. "More than just a providential irony here, there's a lesson to be learned. Horton journeyed the mountain for gold, met the bear, and died. You journeyed the mountain for Christian enlightenment, met the bear, and lived. Your path was blessed, his was not."

Cowboy looked at the bear pelt tied to the packsaddle. That lesson, with all its paradox, would not be lost on him. He watched the preacher mount his horse and settle into the saddle. They shook hands with warmth, each wondering whether their paths would cross again in this lifetime. Brother Van spoke first. "The Lord forgave your sins and made the gift of salvation; never doubt that," he said. "Forgive yourself. What's done is done. Find this man you've wronged. Ask his forgiveness. Whether he does or not, you're righteous with the Almighty." Before Cowboy could reply, Brother Van nudged the dappled pony to a walk and led the pack horse into the meadow, headed north. Over his shoulder, the preacher shouted, "Remember, it will not be your gift until you accept it first." A brief wave of the hand gripping the reins, a nod of the head, and Brother Van fixed his attention on the trek to the winter tribal lands.

Cowboy watched him go until the man and horses were most the way across the meadow. He stowed the cartridge boxes in the saddle bag and lashed the big buffalo gun to his scabbard with strips of leather. Cowboy turned in time to see the preacher reach the bend in the trail as it disappeared into the tree line. His heart felt heavy – and at the same time very happy.

Cowboy twisted in almost a full circle so that he could survey the horizon in all directions. He studied what he could see of the sky. Unlike the plains, the other mountain tops surrounding him kept him from seeing at much distance; barely more than the blue expanse overhead. Brother Van had advised him not to delay his leaving. Big weather was headed their way. Cowboy could see no indication, but he trusted the preacher's caution.

"You know Dusty," he said. "When I was wedged in that cave being troubled by the bear, and you was off to parts unknown, I began to suspect that riding all this way was some fool's errand." Cowboy heaved himself in the saddle. "But the words that man spoke has made me think on my worries with a whole new mind." He smiled from the heart. "It helps to ease the spirit, and it sure-fire gives me *mucho que pensar*, a lot to ponder. But then, amigo, it's a long way back to Texas." Cowboy spurred the big horse.

They loped the trail together at an easy pace.

Their journey had begun.

Bison's Dilemma
Study Questions

1. Cowboy had heard the words of the Bible his whole life, but told Brother Van that he was still missing something. What is the difference in knowing something to be true and believing it? What was Cowboy missing that kept him from finding the peace that Ray had?

2. Brother Van urged him to step out in faith, like the bison in the Bison's Dilemma, and stop wallowing in refusing to forgive himself. How does God's forgiveness of our past free us to walk with him in the present? Have you ever been in a place where you couldn't forgive yourself even though God had forgiven you? What did you do about it?

3. Acts 13:39 says that, through Jesus, "everyone who believes is freed from everything from which you could not be freed by the law of Moses." What does it mean to be truly freed from our attempts to reach God by our own efforts? How can we have a relationship with God if it doesn't come through our own work?

4. Cowboy discovered that God had uniquely blessed his journey, by preserving his life and leading him to Brother Van at just the right time. How do you see God's work in bringing you to where you are now? Do you think God has been leading in your path? Why or why not?

Never Seen His Face

A horse with an empty saddle wandering the trail alone, and no rider in sight, spells trouble. The man might have been pitched when his pony's foot found the gopher hole. Or possibly he tumbled when he leaned east at the time his hoss jack-knifed south. Likely the man got his spine wrinkled in the process. As a result, he lived out a cowboy's great fear: being left afoot. Injured, lame, stove-up, or worse; at the very least, the man ended up miles away from where he wanted to be. Now, shame-faced, he had to walk on thin-soled boots just to get back there.

Cowboy eyed the Claybank mare that stopped nibbling tall thread grass to eye him back. He sat saddle on Dusty, resting at a spot where the crest of the ridge they'd just topped opened on to an expanse of sage flats.

The land there held sparse collections of two-needle pinyons mixed in with juniper trees, copious amounts of black sage, and a sprinkling of Indian paintbrush. Undulating low hills with frequent exposed rock outcroppings stretched in almost a straight line to the south where the start of the plains met the edge of the mountains.

The mare's coloring looked a lighter shade of a red dun in the day's diffused lighting. Her feet showed four white stockings above the hooves, and a cob webbing of dark-ringed marks surrounded the cowlick swirl on the forehead. She carried a single-barreled pumpkin saddle on top of a thin gray blanket evidencing too much gap above the withers. Her plain headstall of the bridle attached to a short one-piece California reins. Something seldom seen this far east. Cowboy judged from the undersized saddle, the lone cinch, and impractical leathers, the rider must be a "show about." What old ranch hands out here call the dude wranglers. This rig was never meant for working cattle.

That thought of some green pea lost down along these mountain trails made Cowboy shake his head in sheer frustration. His quick scan of the surroundings did not uncover a single lost soul ambling off in any direction. Nor could he tell how long or from which direction the mare had been traveling. It puzzled him even more that no bedroll or saddle bags were joined to the mare's rump.

Before Cowboy could explore this unexpected circumstance further, he knew he'd need to take a closer look at the mare and rig. Pressing his left knee into Dusty's side, the buckskin eased two steps forward. The Claybank pricked both ears forward, aiming them at the big stallion approaching her. She let go a quiet whinny, but did not bolt or retreat. Cowboy saw alertness, not skittishness in her manner. Just the same, with movements of deliberate slowness he unstrapped the lariat from his saddle. At the same time he turned Dusty almost perpendicular to the mare so that the buckskin's body hid the coil of a fast loop Cowboy shook out with his free hand.

For minutes Cowboy, Dusty, and the mare stood motionless except for blinking and breathing. A fresh wind blustered in from the west. It blew occasional gusts ahead of the threatening purple clouds Cowboy could see racing their way from the horizon.

As the wrangler knew she would, the Claybank turned her head slightly away from the other two so she could eyeball some new distraction kicking up from that other direction. Cowboy swung one quick whirl at his side, then up over his head and releasing it in a single motion. The rope flattened, landing straight down over the mare's head almost at the same time she saw it coming. Cowboy almost never missed when he threw the hooley-ann. He spun the rope a turn or two around the saddle horn, but aside from a short head shake the mare never as much as flinched.

The occasional spattering of rain that splashed the sandy ground between irregular clumps of grasses came faster now. Each weighty drop pelting his exposed skin made itself felt like Cowboy was being tapped with the stub end of a heavy rope.

Pulling the slicker from the saddle behind him, the wrangler could see dense sheets of the darkening downpour headed his direction. A cold and wet soaking would make the ride back to Texas seem even that much longer. He wagered his oilcloth would be no match for the unfolding downpour. Brother Van had said it right about the storm.

To his left, at a distance of about seventy yards, a rock overhang jutted out almost touching a dead pinyon. Cowboy figured it to be wide and deep enough to shelter himself and the two horses from the encroaching deluge. He made one last scan of the basin for the owner of the Claybank mare he now pulled behind him by the rope. His view now made smaller by the driving rainstorm close at hand.

A line of rock debris edged any entry into the overhang. Fallen from the ledge above, the stones varied from being larger than a wagon's wheel to looking no bigger than a blacksmith's box. Cowboy let Dusty pick the path through the rubble, and trusted that the mare would follow them without much fuss. Once out of the rain, the wrangler saw that this shelter was nothing more than thick strata of dense rock – one part providing the roof, the other forming a bare floor, narrow back wall, and a shallow partial side wall. The soil that had once been a layer wedged in between, now became an unexplained empty space. The broken top of the pinyon, gray and missing its bark, lay together with dozens of dried cones, collected splintered branches, and a jagged heaping of needles strewn along the rocky floor.

The rain continued to pound the prairie as Cowboy unsaddled Dusty and wrapped the woven leather hobble on each foreleg, between fetlock and knee. It was tight enough to keep the stallion from wandering, but loose enough to let him break free if there were real danger. The mare presented a different problem to the cowman. He did not have the second hobble. Although one could be twisted in a lariat quick enough.

Instead Cowboy looped the Claybank's reins over the stout end of the pinyon top. Before removing her saddle, he used the spread of his hand to measure the mare's face and jaw. Then he loosed the long rope from the mare's neck, unrolling it almost completely with an underhand throw. Cowboy doubled it back so he could gauge its span. He used half the length to tie a series of double overhand knots the way he'd been taught on the trail. Frankie called these quick fastenings blood knots, but Ray preferred to dub them barrel loops. In a quarter hour and two adjustments later, Cowboy finished with his new sagebrush hackamore. Now the mare wouldn't have to fight the bit all night. Neither would she merely mosey away.

There had not been the time to graze the animals before taking shelter, and now twenty feet separated them from the closest grass. Even if some horses preferred standing in a steady rain, Cowboy decided to let them feed after first light. He busied himself packing some apple-sized stones into a rough circle near one wall where it formed a rough corner. That he filled with a mound of old cones hollowed out and stuffed with handsful of dry needles Cowboy scooped from the floor. This pile he covered with broken limbs, snapping longer ones to fit inside the rocks. Lighting the kindling with a match from his vest pocket, he soon had a proper fire going.

Cowboy huddled near the flames, listening to the rain slacken and torrent up again as he waited with practiced patience for the rocks to crackle. Then they would radiate heat as well. Warmth already began to bounce back to him off the rock wall. Cowboy knew that he had not the energy to make coffee. He believed it would be sufficient to just gnaw on the sourdough Brother Van had given him and chew on some smoked meat the man also supplied.

First though, Cowboy wanted to dwell a moment on thoughts the preacher had discussed with him. The wrangler also felt the need to read a bit of Scripture before he drowsied off into inattention.

He took the leather-bound book from the coat and placed it next to his knee. For a brief moment, Cowboy leaned back to let the wall support him. He felt shoulders start to slump. The lower back muscles began to relax next. A moment more and the rigors of the long ride jumbled against the turmoil of Cowboy grasping Brother Van's unvarnished guidance. These competing needs fell together ever-so-slow, like some campfire ladle stirring an iron pot of thick stew. The wrangler closed his eyes without thinking.

He stopped fighting it, and in a moment more gave in to the slumber.

* * *

As though poked with a burning stick, Cowboy bolted upright where he sat on the uneven rock floor. The fire still blazed inside the now blackened circle of rocks. It threw off great light. Even in that clear brightness, Cowboy knew he dreamed what now stood before him. A man; bearded, generous face, and eyes that held his own as though tethered. It was those eyes, although composed and gentle, that pierced right into Cowboy's heart. Past that, they looked down into the core of his soul. The wrangler realized he looked into the face of Christ Jesus himself.

Cowboy heard those first words spoken. They came to him in a clear sound, despite the steady rain. He jolted once more, when he realized their meaning. "You know my name," Cowboy said.

"I know all of my Father's children," came the soft reply. "You are my brother, for we are both sons of God." The eyes now embraced Cowboy with an earnestness the wrangler could almost touch. Those eyes gazed a moment at Dusty dozing alongside the mare before turning back to the wrangler wedged against the jagged wall. "Hear this," the voice said. "I have already paid the price; your sins are forgiven. Fear you not." His lean hand swept until it indicated the ponies. "You have journeyed far," the clear voice said again. "But now you must travel back, as the prodigal returns to the home he once left." An approving smile formed on slender lips. "Tell them all what I have done for you this night."

Before Cowboy could form the words to speak again, he felt exhaustion engulf him once more. With a hand still clutching the Bible, he fell into a bottomless, transforming, and now dreamless sleep.

* * *

It surprised Cowboy not one bit that the sun hung a foot or more above the far horizon. He woke to the clumsy sounds of the big buckskin blowing repeatedly and stomping his hooves with some impatience. "I swear, Dusty," Cowboy told his horse. "You're noisier than a painted cat when you ain't been fed. Or are you just in a lather to hotfoot it down the trail; me straight-legging all the way and shaking hands with grandma, too?" Cowboy laughed as he moved to stand. He shook off the dirt he'd gathered during the night, placed the book thoughtfully back in his coat, and turned his attention to the ponies.

Foregoing his usual meager breakfast makings, Cowboy pitched the saddle on the Claybank, cinching it only loosely. He left the halter secured to her jaw, but tied the all-but-useless fancy bridle to the saddle's horn. He knew, even with his back turned and without seeing, that Dusty watched all this with big dark eyes assessing his each movement. "Your turn, big fella," Cowboy said. For a moment he stroked the withers and rump. He checked as he did every morning for signs of anything that needed tending before unhobbling the legs and tacking up.

"You was there last night when the dream come on me," Cowboy said. He removed the bit before sliding the bridle on so Dusty could graze and still be held by the reins. "It was some powerful, what I saw. Clear as anything," he confided, putting on the woven blanket and the saddle. "Like the bewildered folks in Scripture, the Lord spoke to me - not no one else. Jesus spoke just to me." Cowboy stood without moving. He held the cinch's end in his hand, yet to be tightened and buckled. "I never seen his face before that moment. Drawings in church and the Good Book aplenty, but never his actual face." Dusty relaxed twitching ears. He stuck his head back a bit, jutting out the jaw, as if to agree.

Cowboy led the pair from under the overhang, reins in one hand, halter's rope in the other. He stopped at a spot where the thread grass bunched together in large clusters. While Dusty and the mare devoured thick green shoots easily pulled from the soggy soil, Cowboy made his way to the top of the hill that gave way to the overhang at its north point.

As he chewed on the vittles he'd set aside for last night's supper, the wrangler turned in a slow circle. His eyes stopped at any tree, shrub, rock, or shadow that might be hiding an injured man. None held his attention for long.

At each point of the compass, Cowboy let out a loud, "Hell-lew." That got him nothing; not so much as an echo in this open flatland. Satisfied after a second turnabout that he done what little he could to find the missing rider, he made his way back to the almost-fed horses. Cowboy indulged them another quarter-hour, then fixed Dusty's bit and pulled himself into the saddle.

He intended to reach the grassland's edge by nightfall. If not by sundown, then by next day's afternoon.

* * *

It troubled Cowboy that for the full three days since leaving the rocky overhang he had kept the river in sight off to his right, but he had yet to pass all the way through the sage plateau. "I don't rightly recall these ragged brush and juniper lands being so extended," he told Dusty. "But if I was to say it true, most ways from leaving Frankie's camp my mind was full and my heart was overflowing." He patted the horse with his reins hand, the woven lead being held in the other. "Good thing you can follow a trail by your lonesome." He turned around part way to look at the Claybank that followed quietly at the end of the long rope. She had occupied his thoughts a great deal since they found her. The wrangler knew pulling her like this all the way to Texas would involve more work than just riding Dusty. Since he had yet to sit saddle on her, Cowboy could not judge the mare's worth as a mount. "Maybe I'll give you to Emma as a surprise," he told the mare. "Or maybe I'll sell you and that fancy rig first town I come to has money." The mare gave no reaction to his words the way the buckskin usually did. She merely looked off in the distance while he talked. Cowboy just shook his head at this lack of manners. To his way of thinking, this horse was not uneasy near people. But neither did she much cotton to them either. She responded to all his directions by rote, like some horse-haired machine. He'd yet to see the tiniest spark of spirit displayed in anything she did. "Leading a red-hided ghost back to Atascosa ain't my first idea of something needs doin'," he told the Claybank before facing back around.

The sun had arced its way almost to overhead, now free of clouds that covered most of the morning's skies. The brightness coming with it caused Cowboy to squint as he scanned the sage looking for what he remembered to be a stout juniper thicket, no broader than thirty-feet. A single twin-needle pine stood apart by half that distance. It towered above the loamy ground. In between, the trail began its descent down into the rolling grasslands.

In the glare, he could not see any trees grouped in that fashion. Tugging down the Stetson's brim, Cowboy shaded his face enough for him to see without slitting eyes. What he gained in shade, he lost in vision. The hat blocked what was to be seen then at the distance. Grabbing the Stetson's crown and pulling it loose, Cowboy held it at extended arms-length. It blocked the sun once more, but he now saw the horizon. There, in the distance he picked out a thicket located near a lone tree. The pine seemed shorter than he recalled. He would know soon enough. On the way up-trail, Cowboy notched it with his knife. The trail mark would confirm he traveled the right path.

Less than two hours later Dusty, Cowboy, and the mare started down the trail's narrow decline. Before them, stretching from horizon east to that of horizon west, an unending set of gentle hills rose and fell. The continuous grass undulated, blown by a west wind. "Yippee-yai, Dusty," Cowboy yelled with pent-up enthusiasm borne of relief. "That's the prairie that stretches all the way back to Amarillo." His grin did not stretch from one ear to the other, but neither did it miss by much.

Ahead of them on the trail, Cowboy saw the same puzzlement that had intrigued him weeks before. For reasons not obvious to the wrangler, a lesser trail spur angled off to the grassland in a steep and rock-strewn path. Cowboy followed the route of this pathway with narrowed eyes. He soon realized that near where the path met the grass, a herd of twenty or so grazing *mesteño* ponies stood watching him. The mustangs looked every bit the feral strays the Spaniards name them for: high necks, sloping shoulders, narrow muzzles, and low-set tails. Their colorings ranged from black to bay, chestnut to pinto, and variations typical of their kind. What could not be missed was the prominent black stallion that walked to place himself between the ponies and

Cowboy. Chest full out and neck arched, this dominant male of the herd looked at the two horses on the hillside, not the wrangler. The stallion whinnied long and high-pitched. Dusty replied only by pointing both ears in the herd's direction. The mare whinnied back, moving up beside Cowboy as she did so. The Claybank apparently wanted an unobstructed view. Cowboy could see the beginnings of excitement flicker in her eyes. "Well now," he said in tones of understanding. "It's a genuine stud hoss that gets the life in to you."

Cowboy climbed down, pulling the slack out of the mare's lead rope. He stepped closer to the Claybank to better judge her reaction. From over her shoulder he gazed more fully at the prancing stallion. His coat glistened, unmarked by any other color. The black stretched from nose to tail. Given its ample size, Cowboy guessed it to be out of true Irish draught horse stock. How such an animal as this came to be here on these Great Plains seemed a mystery to him. But the stallion loomed big enough to dominate any contest for mares in the herd. Cowboy delighted that Dusty showed no interest in besting him.

Without warning, the mare nickered a mournful call. Cowboy could feel the tug against the rope in his hand. The wrangler made a quick decision. He tossed a stirrup over the seat. In seconds he had the mare's cinch undone. The saddle fell to the rocks in the path in a thump. A moment more and the halter slid over her ears and off the jaw. He raised an arm above his head so as to quirt the Claybank on the rump with the rope. He stopped. If the mare was to go, the choice must be hers alone.

She gave Cowboy not so much as a final look. The mare stumbled, with focused determination, down the rocky path. She stopped a good ten feet from where the stallion trotted out to greet her. They eyed each other for long seconds before the bigger horse stepped up, neck arched, flared nostrils an inch from hers. For more than a minute they both inhaled each other's breath. Satisfied that he knew her smell, the stallion turned to rejoin the gathered mustangs. Carefully, the stud kept himself between the herd and this new stranger.

The stallion gave a signal that Cowboy did not see, and at this distance could not hear. In a rush, the herd bolted headlong toward the west. The Claybank trailed not far behind. Before the stampede crossed the small rise, Cowboy caught one last glimpse of the Claybank's face. He swore he saw her smiling.

Having stepped himself down the lesser trail a pace or two, Cowboy turned back to find himself eyeball to eyeball with the buckskin. "Is there a name for that look?" he asked Dusty. "'Cuz I already know what you're thinking." He looked to see the trampled grass the mustangs left behind. He wondered how long the herd would take to include the Claybank. Looking at Dusty again, he said, "I'm just a cowpuncher raised down in Texas, but even I can calculate this out." He held up an index finger for the horse to see. "First, Brother Van ministers to me at the cabin." He raised the second finger. "Next, I have the dream where Jesus speaks to me." He raised the third. "And just now, the Claybank rejoins her own kind so she can run the prairie the rest of her days on the mustang's journey." Bemusement wrinkled into a weak smile. "I know it's time to go. Not just to Texas, but back home to family in Atascosa." He shook his head as his eyes focused on nothing. "It's been too long and I'm tired of running."

From the range coat pocket, Cowboy took his small Bible with one hand. He held reins and the Stetson he'd removed in the other. "I feel moved at this moment to read verse before we head out." It surprised him some when the Scriptures fell open at pages separated by some kind of dried leaf. Cowboy recognized it at last as Narrow Leaf Cottonwood. Brother Van had a stack of them piled on the cabin's side table. "I don't remember the preacher doing this," he told Dusty. "There must be a passage here in the Book of Luke he wanted me to read." Cowboy ran a long finger over the left page and halfway down the right.

The searching stopped when his eyes fell upon the words: "Return home and tell them how much God has done for you. So the man went away and told all over town how much Jesus had done for him."

Cowboy returned the hat to his head. He looked over a shoulder trying to spot the mountains they had descended from. At this distance, the peaks were barely a blur. The wrangler studied them anyway for a long moment. He could not imagine riding further north into the high snow country this late in the year. Certainly not doing so with such determined intention, but that was Brother Van's path, not his. He expected that his own would be the more difficult.

Cowboy heaved himself on Dusty's back. He used both hands on the saddle's horn and no stirrups, mounting up like some young buckaroo. "We don't need to ride the wagon tongue this time, *mi caballo*, to point rightly toward Atascosa County." He patted the buckskin's shoulder with a gentle touch. "Texas is that-a-way."

Cowboy nodded at the far horizon, turning the big horse until they headed south. Tapping a boot heel, he nudged Dusty to a canter.

They loped the trail at an easy pace.

Their journey home had begun.

Never Seen His Face
Study Questions

1. When Cowboy saw Jesus in his dream, Jesus said that they were brothers. Brothers share in the same inheritance. What does it mean to be a brother of Jesus? Are you a brother of Jesus? How does knowing that change how you view where you are now and where you are going?

2. Cowboy had a dramatic dream, encountering Jesus. Not everyone has that same experience. What are some other ways you can be sure that you are following Jesus? How does the Bible show us what God is saying to us, even if we don't have a dream of our own?

3. The Claybank joined the mustangs and found something familiar. Through the dream, seeing the Claybank, and the verse he read, Cowboy knew he had to stop running and go back home, no matter what he might face there. What have you been running from that you need to return to? What do you need to make right from your past? How do you plan to do that?

4. As Cowboy recognized, his journey from the beginning had been led by God to bring him back home again. All of his adventures along the way pointed to that conclusion, as he calculated out. How has God been leading our journey? What are the people, places, and events that have brought you to where you are now? What steps do you need to take to walk with Jesus on the journey he has for you?

PART 3

Coming Home

All That Glitters

Pi-a-wa-oo, the Comanche call them. They might travel in pairs, but the mountain lion always hunts alone. Seldom seen, these quiet predators fell their prey with deadly leaps from boulder tops or drops from leafy trees. A cougar's print is unmistakable: tear-shaped toes, one front digit extending past the other. No trace of claw. And, the heavy three-lobed heel leaves a distinct impression. Unlike any man on the run, a mountain lion never tries to cover its tracks.

Looking down now at the deep footmarks pressed in muddy snow next to the trail, Cowboy wondered why the big cat had made its way this close to the caprock of the *Llano Estacado*, that palisaded plain of the Texas Panhandle. From where he sat saddle on Dusty, it still required more than three weeks ride, in good weather, to reach this critter's Trans Pecos hunting grounds. Down there, plentiful deer and countless "skunk pigs" roam the rough terrain, providing ample food supply.

It didn't take a tracker's eye to see the panther's path meandered east a bit before disappearing behind some slight rise, now topped with vestiges of melting snow. Before long, if the ache in Cowboy's broken knuckle gave any foretelling, the black-and-purple sky behind him held another of the season's Blue Northers. Darkness stretched the whole length of the rugged escarpment over his shoulder, covering most of the horizon. The storm rushed to dump heavy rain, wet snow, or both along the wrangler's path. That same small rise he gazed upon likely would be buried in the process.

"Glad we quit the high table-lands, Dusty," he said to the buckskin. "Hardly what I'd call habitable. Nary a tree or bush, nor much in the way of water. 'Cepting the occasional seep or a *pozo* at the bottom of some coulee. And too few springs to count." Cowboy looked back for a moment the way they had come. "Animals shun it for good reason," he continued. "Even the tribes crossed there in only two or three special places." The rider pulled the range coat collar tighter against unceasing wind blowing cold against his back. "It's so flat, doubtful you could hear a single echo in that whole expanse between the Canadian River and the Colorado."

Cowboy reined Dusty to a stop when he saw the thin wisp of smoke eking from a broken chimney. Tucked to the wall at the canyon's opening, a dog-run cabin anchored a shabby homestead. Beside it, a barn of no great size stood, attached to a small corral of somewhat questionable construction.

Through the slats in the mesquite fence, six pairs of narrowed eyes watched the horse and rider approach. Instead of searching for more food scraps in the clapboard trough or spending time rooting through the corral's loose dirt, the young hogs huddled tightly in the farthest corner. All heads faced outward, as if this afforded them considerable more protection.

"These swine is more than a mite skittish," Cowboy said to the back of Dusty's ears. Stepping down from the saddle, the rider paused to look at the porkers more closely. "Wonder if them paw prints is what got 'em so spooked out here in the middle of big lonesome?"

Before Cowboy could begin to speculate on that, a voice called out from the breezeway of the cabin, "What do *you* want?"

The tone clearly matched the unwelcoming look on the woman's face. Standing in the corridor centered atwixt the two lodging compartments, a small figure stood with one hand balled on the hip and the other held to her eyes shading them against the wind and blowing bits of dust. A double-hammer Colt shotgun leaned against the cabin wall next to her feet. Cowboy noticed that both hammers were already cocked.

The wrangler removed his hat as he led Dusty the few steps it took to reach the porch. "Afternoon, miss," he said, looking into her all-but-glaring eyes. "I mean you no harm. I'm just a lone *baccaro* headed..."

He didn't get to finish.

The woman cut him off without warning, "It's missus to you." The scowl boring down at him looked out of place coming from eyes the color of good whiskey. It did little to remove doubt as to her exact wedded status in the midst of this open territory.

"Beg pardon, ma'am," he said with guarded warmth. Cowboy replaced the big hat on his head. "I intend no bother to you or yours. Just a horse and rider headed south to Atascosa County for the spring."

He jerked a thumb over his shoulder at the darkened sky, but kept his eye on her and the loaded scattergun. "Big gust front's comin'. I'd be much obliged just to bed down in your barn 'til this blizzard blows itself out tonight."

He half-turned to assay that tiny structure's actual capacity hold both him and the horse together. Satisfied, he set his attention on the woman once more.

In Cowboy's experience, he found it an easier chore to judge the worth of an unknown *cayuse* than to figure a woman at first meeting. This one certainly would take more than a single glance. He already reckoned by her abrupt manner that she had not been raised in Texas. The woman spoke her words with an accent sounding Southern in origin, but clipped from living in a grand city somewhere. That made the rarity of her unmistakable beauty even more unexpected out here on this isolated homestead.

Cowboy guessed her no more than five feet tall when barefoot. A Cupid's bow mouth enclosed lips neither full nor thin. Her constant biting the lower one made it hard for him to tell. A waist no more than a hand's breadth, down to which hung the ponytail of sleek black hair. The skin's smooth pallor evidenced little exposure to harsh sun. Cowboy judged her certainly no clodhopper's wife, but a most handsome woman just the same.

"What is it, Prudence?" The man's rich baritone did not match his skinny frame as he stepped up behind her. He stood head and shoulders taller than she. Cowboy's eyes were at once drawn to the bulky wrapping of burlap that extended from elbow to knuckles on his right arm. Thin twine, loosely knotted, barely held the sacking in place.

"This man's likely here to steal one of our pigs, Isaac." the woman said. "He certainly looks hungry enough." She held up the shotgun for her husband to take. "Shoot him now, and be done with it."

Isaac shook his head at her while laughing quietly. "You know we can't do that. Not the neighborly thing to do in these parts. Besides, can't be sure I could handle this coach gun with just the one hand." He cast a weak smile in Cowboy's direction, embarrassment touching his jaw. Holding up his unencumbered good palm, Isaac assured the wrangler. "I'm not even left-handed."

"I swear to you, Isaac Coverdale," she said in a quick huff. "Sometimes you are a lean-witted hempseed." Through clenched teeth, Prudence hissed out a long breath that ended in resignation. "Why not just tell this tall stranger that you haven't the means to protect yourself—or me—on this rundown excuse of a farmstead." Prudence propped the gun back against the rough wall. "I did not follow you," she said, "all the way out here from Memphis to die of pneumonia in some drafty cabin. I care not that it belonged to your family."

The sound of her stomping away reverberated in that tiny hallway, punctuated by the creaking of hinges and the crash of wood on wood as the door slammed shut. Both men stared at the cracked flimsy jambs, just waiting for each to crumble from that hard smashing.

"You'll have to forgive her, but my wife has been most poorly of late," Isaac said. "I'm afraid the long journey out here, only to find these conditions…," His good hand swept the breadth of the tiny homestead. "It fairly well broke what was left of her spirit."

Cowboy noted the mix of surrender and regret in the thin man's eyes as the homesteader now studied rough planking at his feet. But the wrangler also recognized a streak of determination beginning to stretch across the other man's features. In all, Cowboy judged him to be a tough hombre; at the moment, standing on the short side of bad luck.

"How'd you come to these parts?" Cowboy asked. "It's a far piece just from here to Redwater, near the shoals you ford the river into Arkansas. And a whole mite further to reach the actual Mississip'."

Isaac began to nurse the bundled arm with fingers of his free hand. He winced with the first touch, and grimaced at the second. "It began with her cousin, Charlie, the sailor. He was down on the ships near the Isle of Cuba. Came home by way of New Orleans." The man looked off to nothing in particular in the near distance. "The Federals panicked over yellow fever coming out of Havana and Santiago. Blockaded the Mississippi north to protect towns along the river." Isaac sat on the stoop, gently resting the bad arm on his knees. "Young Charlie jumped ship and made his way back to Memphis overland. He didn't look that sick when he got home; but folks that could, fled the city when they heard he was there. Including us, after he died."

Cowboy stepped up almost knee to knee with Isaac. "That ain't no dogfall. What calamity has happened here?" He asked, pointing down at the burlap and string.

"This is Providence's way of telling me that I should have remained a gentlemen's banker," Isaac said. "I can no longer cling to the notion that mere visits to a farm as a youth are the same as growing up there." His voice rose to be heard above the freshening wind. It blew harder, carrying with it the smell of impending rain. Isaac could tell that the tall stranger in the broad hat had not gathered the meaning of his words.

"Every spring and summer," the thin man continued, "the family would visit Uncle Harold's one-hundred-and-sixty acres near Robinsonville on the Arkansas side. My two sisters and I would help out with the milking and feeding, alongside our cousins." Cowboy could see that the man had much fondness for this memory. "Uncle would take us boys hunting for one thing or another. We always came home with meat for the pot." Isaac grinned as if that would explain everything. "Why, once or twice I even helped my Uncle make repair to some of the farm buildings. That included applying fresh plaster between the planks of the old smoke house. Much like I was attempting to do here."

Isaac pointed with a long finger to the cabin's logs near the roof. Along the top two rows where dried mortar should have been, only a darkened emptiness remained. Cowboy nodded at the sight, but the other man only shook his head. "I don't understand the thinking here," Isaac said in genuine puzzlement. "Why leave them open all this time when the cabin was finished years ago?"

Cowboy held back his laugh, but he did blurt out a quick breath. "You was too late to summer here," he said. "These mesquite shanties can warm up like a Dutch oven under the hot Texas sun. Homesteaders chip out them spaces for airing heat and patch it back in time for the chinking season of late fall." The wrangler grinned barely half a smile. "You just started considerable late, is all. That how you got the arm?"

Before Isaac could answer, large flakes of wet slush began to pelt both men. Wind blew strong enough to start a faint whine in the distance. The pitch only increased as gusts roared up the canyon past the cabin. Isaac rose, careful not to jostle his wrapped arm.

"Setting out the tools needed to begin this patch work, I fell backwards over a water bucket only to land on a ditching spade handle. A very stout handle, mind you. This is the result." He raised the bad arm. "Broke it, I think. Hurts like the Dickens."

Squinting eyes almost shut, Isaac turned to face west. He said, "Light's almost gone and the weather is upon us. Take your shelter there in the barn, such as it is." He shook his head at the thought. "It should do to keep the wind off you, but not much else. We'll talk more tomorrow." He turned to walk through the same doorway his wife had slammed that short while before.

Cowboy nodded his thanks. Taking Dusty by the reins, he led the buckskin into the tiny structure. Clearly, the wrangler heard no offer of a hot meal. Neither had he been given the excuse for not doing so. Plain bad manners. Feeding strangers, even meagerly, was a long-held tradition on the range. In his heart, Cowboy knew that he likely carried more food in his saddle bags than the Coverdales had in their cabin's larder. He pondered how he should treat that situation come morning. The storm would have blown itself out by then.

***

The sun had yet to fully clear the canyon wall. It sparkled off what few flakes that still clung to the cabin roof. The moaning wind had persisted deep into the night, long after it had dumped the brief but heavy snow. Slush stood pushed up against the windward side of cabin and barn. It piled as high as Cowboy's knees. Now, a steady mildness set in as calm covered the open land. Any wind still moving felt less than a breeze on the wrangler's face.

Cowboy walked with careful strides through the mud as he steered Dusty past the corner of the tiny barn. He held bridle leathers in one hand, his rifle in the other. It surprised him to find Isaac in a somewhat formal coat, long and pitch black in color as the night before had been. The man sat on a worn wooden crate just outside the barn's door. He had both elbows resting on thighs, the good arm raised to cradle his face deep in a narrow palm. Cowboy thought it a pitiful sight.

Isaac started at the appearance of stranger and horse. In a split second his face eased off desperation to show relief. "I...I..." was all he mustered before pushing himself off the box.

"Thought I'd hightailed it out of here without so much as paying my respects?" Cowboy laughed. "You don't know my Ma and how me and my brothers was brought up. Manners is most important back in Atascosa." The wrangler looked at the other man's attire more closely, wondering whether they considered these actual farm duds in Mississippi. "You're a mite dressed up to help me skin this deer."

At those words, Isaac noticed Dusty's burden for the first time. In place of the bedroll and that small extra saddle the buckskin usually carried, the carcass of a large male deer lay strapped across the rump. Its long white tail rested unmoving atop the nearest saddlebag. Examining it more closely, the man could see only the tips of antlers pointing away from him on the other side. He saw, too, that thin mist clinging to its tawny hide as the last escaping warmth met cool morning's air.

"When I spoke of hunting to you last evening," Isaac said in halting tones. "I might not have told that part where only Uncle Harold himself dressed and processed all the meat." The man swallowed hard once, lost some coloring in his cheeks, but could not bring himself to look away.

"Ain't no never mind," Cowboy replied. He led his big horse closer to the barn's door. Over his shoulder, he confided to Isaac, "I just got this pure hankering for some tasty *barbacoa*, meat slow seared over hot mesquite coals. I'd seen fresh deer tracks along the mouth of the canyon afore the storm blew in. Figured they'd hunker down and wait the weather out just like me and Dusty." The wrangler pointed in the direction of far-off brush tops. "They was only a mile or so down the way."

Isaac watched from a safe distance as Cowboy tossed his lariat over a low barn rafter. In a minute, the tall cowman maneuvered Dusty into position and used the rope to suspend the deer. Held tight by the hind hooves, it hung a good foot or so off the dirt floor.

"I calculate that mostly you're a city boy," Cowboy began. "Seems like it or not, circumstance has fated you of late to become a plow chaser." The wrangler swung his head in a slow circle. "Don't see much crops or silage set aside anywheres. Them swine must account for most of your actual food stuffs." Cowboy squinted in the direction of the still-huddled pigs. "I don't figure you for a man who can cut up a hog with much ease, let alone render any lards." He turned back to level his gaze at the thin man. A deep stillness filled the gap between them. The cowboy's face took on a look that bent between quietude and menace. "But for the sake of you and your woman, it's a skill that means survival out here. *Sabe*?"

Isaac stared for a full second before nodding, but he spoke no words. Cowboy's lips softened into a quick smile, but his eyes held little mirth. "Just keep an eye on what I do. You got six chances out there in the pen to get it right." He drew the long blade from its sheath on his belt. "I expect as the missus might fancy some stew meat and shank steaks for fixin's. We best get after it."

Cowboy ran a light thumb along the knife's edge. He frowned a bit, then allowed himself to grin showing full teeth. "Besides," he said. "Possible it will take a spell longer to sharpen this old *chuchillo* here than to do the actual skinning."

It did.

It also took some time to crumble up salt lumps found in a tight-lidded clay jar. That stout pottery squatted in a corner of the barn until Cowboy moved it to lay out his bedroll. He showed Isaac how to rub the seasoning vigorously top and bottom onto the meat just cut.

"You're going to need," the wrangler said, "to cut these gunny sacks to strips. Then wrap 'em tight around each chunk of venison." While the man did so, Cowboy drug the crate into the barn and began packing meat bundles inside the box. "This'll keep vermin and such from being tempted," he said.

Isaac hustled about to complete the chore. On the man's face Cowboy could see the faintness of a childlike joy. In his mind, the younger man must be reliving Uncle Harold's farm visits or maybe he was just grateful not to face certain starvation. When Isaac finished packing the crate, Cowboy said, "It's a nuisance we ran out of salt. Get you some store-bought in town, and cure what meat's left she don't cook up right away. This weather, it should keep you to the end of spring."

The first dark cloud of the morning passed over Isaac's face. "I'm not certain the folks at the general store will accommodate that," he said. "We're well in debt to them as it is. Mr. Kessler advanced us the purchase of the twelve pigs two months ago. Plus he obliged us these few provisions we've been living off of." His voice trailed down to a near whisper as he finished.

Cowboy knew a confession like that, for someone of his once lofty position, could bash the man's pride completely. "Living on the tick," the wrangler said, "is a darn tough row to hoe. Done so myself in younger days, vexing 'til I got out from under." For no apparent reason that Isaac could see, Cowboy nodded to himself. The puncher had made a decision to that unsettled quandary rolling over and again in the back of his mind. To the other man he simply said, "It's near mid-morning and I'm settin' out at first light. We best get to chinking them logs, if we're to get you any relief from that wind."

***

The sun hung halfway to dusk by the time the two men stopped to move chinking gear to a new spot. That assortment consisted of a bucket holding remnants of clay dug from the hillside, broken dried twigs, and melted snow; the ditching spade; and a wooden churn Cowboy stood on to reach high spots on the open logs.

Admiring their labor thus far, Cowboy swept his hand in the direction of the finished wall. "My Ma would tell us long about now, 'Boys, it's a thing of *purty*.'" Isaac had to agree, proud of the work even if he only sloshed the bucket contents around one-handed with the broad shovel. "To my recollection," Cowboy said, "You ain't spoke of how come you by this place? Belong to your kin?"

Before answering that question, the thin man made certain that his wife had not returned with the last bit of clay from the hill. "My folks live in Bald Knob, not that far from my uncle in Robinsonville." he said. "They welcomed us as always and were happy to put us up until the fever scare played out." His gaze shifted toward the approaching woman now struggling to carry her small pail. "That is, they did until they heard how we looked after Charlie until he gave up the ghost. After a spate of shouts and accusations, my father gave us a handful of hard money in a kerchief and the reins to a swayback old nag pulling that whiskey shay over there." Isaac appeared reconciled to this circumstance. "The last thing he did was give me the papers to this place, with the hope that we would not die disheartened out here the way his step-mother had done."

"But mostly, he wanted us gone," Prudence called out from the length of about ten paces. Even at that distance and her husband's low tones, she knew the substance of his words. "That sorry horse died just short of Texarkana," she said. "Bought another one and spent the rest of our money getting here." Prudence handed the pail to Cowboy. Her eyes, less fierce than before, did not leave his face. Finding no answers there, she pulled her shawl tighter and turned to let the sun warm her back.

"I figure it's done in an hour's time," Cowboy said. He helped Isaac mix the final batch of mortar before heaving himself up on the churn once more. The wrangler dolloped plaster into the length of decreasing open space with quick strokes of his makeshift ladle. When all had been filled he stepped down. "This time three days from now, that'll all be dried hard as any caliche slag."

Cowboy found himself facing Prudence eye-to-eye now after she stepped up on the porch. "Why have you done all this?" she asked. Interest rather than scorn held her look this time. "You provided us with sustenance enough to last us through the winter. Now you've kept us from freezing as well. You showed us where to find deadfall firewood down in the canyon and a spring with better water than in our old well." Her eyes moistened slightly, but not quite to tears.

"Weren't much when you think about it, ma'am," the wrangler said. "Raised as I was in Atascosa, this is all in a day's chores for us four brothers."

He turned to help Isaac, already busy cleaning up the clutter. He turned back when Prudence spoke again, "You demand nothing from us in return. Neither have you taken advantage of a crippled man, or his wife." She bent an inch or two toward the wrangler. "There must be *something* that you want."

Cowboy slid the Stetson from his head. "For a fact, ma'am," he said, "there is. Before I take Dusty and ride down the trail," the big man paused, "just once before I go," he paused a second time to affix his most somber look, "I'd like to see you smile."

Caught so unawares by that request, the corners of Prudence's mouth twitched at once. While not a true smile, her face held a mild delight. Isaac could barely hold back his own tears at a sight not seen since Memphis. "Sir," she said to the wrangler, "I will gladly grin like a possum for you. Moreover, I will dance at your wedding, but first please rid us of that cussed catamount savaging our pigs." She softened her eyes in hopeful supplication. "Half of them are gone now. Soon, we'll have nothing to sell in the market next spring."

Cowboy swung around to survey the remaining swine, then looked back at the man, and last at his wife. He grinned now, more smirk than mirth. "I truly 'spect that big cat won't bother you no more."

***

The cougar stopped when he smelled the blood. In another moment, the cat found a heap of deer guts left at the base of the tree. That double mouthful, he gobbled down in big bites as though famished. The light of this night's full moon glimmered off the snow in a brilliant sparkle. That illuminated the feline's fur with a dazzling glow. It outlined the shape of the cat's body unmistakably in the clear night's air.

For a long minute, a rough tongue licked mouth and chin to taste the last of the unexpected morsel. The panther's ever-moving nostrils searched more scent, and found something of interest nearby. This time, it drifted down from a fixed spot between the low-hung limbs.

At a height of about eight feet, remnants of the deer's ribs and part of its skull leaned against the tree's bark, tacked there by a hand-forged nail. Unsatisfied hunger, mixed with curiosity, made the cougar raise up on hind legs to sniff at this next helping of easy food just barely within its extended paw's reach.

Next to the barn, Cowboy used the corral's top rail to balance the Winchester. He steadied the sight on a spot at the base of the skull, between and just below the cat's cocked ears. The wrangler eased out his breath until it was gone. He could feel the curve of the trigger hug the tip of his finger.

At this distance it would be hard to miss.

***

Even if a man can step across it in a single stride, Texans will call it a river. They're just proud to have water running through the countryside. So it was in Cooperville. Cowboy watched the thin trickle eke its way along the ditch to form the settlement's northern perimeter. He hoped the melting snow would eventually give it an actual torrent someday.

The wrangler rode the big horse into town. A fresh set of cougar's claws, wrapped tight in muslin scraps, lay snugged in the over-stuffed saddle bags. In a quick scan, Cowboy noted the five wooden structures that comprised the mercantile establishments; four of them two-story. Not a saloon to be found among them. That seemed surprising to him for a county seat and the only established community for many miles around.

Just past the Wayfarers Hotel, an imposing whitewashed lodging with its wide porch wrapped around the second floor, sat a low, squat, but wide building. The narrow walkway there exhibited a series of tall posts supporting a gabled wooden canopy. Above that, unmistakable bold red lettering proclaimed the words, "Kessler Lumber Company—General Merchandise—Market—Post Office." An old man sat alone in a stiff chair outside the double-door entryway. He watched Cowboy and Dusty approach but appraised neither horse nor rider with his scrutiny. Instead, he fixed his look on the fancy extra saddle tied on the buckskin's rump. The man took note of the matching bridle also fixed along there.

"Hold up there, friend," the older man said to Cowboy. "How come you by that fancy rigging? A bit showy for a working hand."

"For a fact," Cowboy said, "it is." With those few words he let his face go blank, expecting the old man possibly to launch into some serious barter. "I got this for helping a fella up the way find a good outfit for his pony. He couldn't ride no more."

"That right?" the man asked. After a long pause, he continued, "Name's Kessler. My emporium here." He indicated his name painted on the window with a thumb. "Don't much see the likes of that seat, skirt, or strings in these parts. Not seem to suit you or the horse, if you don't mind my saying." He stared up at the tall rider's eyes, but could read little in them. "Care to parley a trade?"

"What's the offer?"

"You get down to it, don't you?"

Cowboy just stared in reply.

"I'll give you forty dollars for the both of them; silver coin or federal paper."

"That's a start," Cowboy said, almost without moving his lips.

"Don't sour my milk, son; I intend to have those leathers!" Kessler stood now to point at the rig. "We can dicker 'til sundown, and I won't budge above fifty. But I will throw in a dinner over at the wife's cafe. Feed you 'til you're full as a tick: Beefsteak, home fries, biscuits, and my Martha's apple pie. Some grains for the horse, too, if you'll walk him over to the livery."

Cowboy stepped off Dusty to stand in the dirt at the store's sidewalk. He stood face-to-face with the old man and took his hand. "I can set with that, Mr. Kessler," he said. "A duck-on-a-rock if it ain't a fair deal. Saddle's yours, bridle too." The wrangler began to unhitch the rig from his mount.

"Come inside," Kessler said. "We'll settle up."

A low wooden counter ran the length of one wall; its rough milled lumber now rubbed smooth by years of wear. From beneath it, Kessler retrieved an angular metal box stacked atop a cloth-bound journal. Plentiful lined-paper sheets stuck out from its covers. Out of the box the old man counted out the purchase price: twenty-five silver dollars, twenty-five in paper currency. Before shoving the money across the counter to Cowboy, Kessler wet a pencil's tip with his tongue then wrote figures and notes in the journal.

"Big as your mercantile is," Cowboy said, "I'll wager half the county has a page in that tally book of yours."

"In that you would be wrong, stranger." Kessler patted the pages with unbending fingers. "I got the *whole* county in here," he smiled with enormous satisfaction.

"That include them new corn-knockers I met at the canyon mouth about ten miles back? Pretty woman with a slim-as-could-be husband?"

"Ah yes, the Coverdales." Kessler's face clouded at the mere sound of the name. "I told Martha that those two could not cut it out here. Said that lending money to them was a fool's errand." He shook his head at the memory. "But my wife would have none of it. So, those two are down on the page for dry goods, supplies, a dozen pigs, and some feed. I'm letting them raise the herd to market size." In near dejection, the old man flipped the sheets until he got to the Coverdale page. "Doubtful I'll see any of it, but they owe eighteen dollars. And that's with the pigs at a better than fair price."

Cowboy took the two top coins off one the five stacks. Those he put in a coat pocket along with the pile of paper money. The remaining silver dollars he pushed back to a shocked Kessler. "That should square the account and leave them five to the good," the wrangler said.

Looking at the unasked, but obvious question in the old man's face, Cowboy said, "I can't make up for the misfortune that's followed them up 'til now. But I can, at least, stake them to a fightin' chance." Nodding to himself more than Kessler, he finished, "They did me a good turn is all."

Cowboy tipped his hat to the still speechless store owner. "Reckon the café's in the hotel, next building over?" the old man nodded an imperceptible reply as the wrangler left him to stew in his wonderment.

***

It didn't take long to get Dusty started on his helping of feed at the stable. It took Cowboy even less to settle himself at a small table in the somewhat rustic dining room. The Sharps Big Fifty leaned against the wall behind him, next to the Winchester 73. Cowboy's saddlebags draped over the back of the closest chair. From one, both boxes of .50 cal shells sat table top within his reach, almost touching the half-filled coffee cup. An empty china plate held nothing more than gristle and a chunk of bone. He'd left the merest scrap of potato untouched, while the apple pie was completely gone. Only the hanging scent of cinnamon remained.

Cowboy ran two fingers idly along the top and sides of each corrugated box, staring but not seeing the fancy logo printed there. His mindless contemplation stopped when he looked up to the tear-stained face of Prudence Coverdale. "Mr. Kessler said I'd find you here," she said. "Isaac finally came to see Doc McKay about his arm. I went to the store instead to beg more supplies, salt and such. I thought I could buy more time to pay back with this." In her extended palm she held a dented silver dollar. "I saw you slip it into Isaac's coat while he was mixing plaster," she went on. "I took it and never told him anything. I didn't want him to be the one that came to Kessler groveling." Her tears flowed again in great profusion. "I've done you grievously."

Cowboy stood at once. The napkin stayed tucked beneath his chin and spread across his chest. He pulled a chair for her to sit. "Ma'am. There's no need," he began.

"From the beginning," Prudence said, "I have treated you with sniping and distain. I poured anger on you meant for others. I even asked to have you shot." She pulled out an embroidered hanky from a sleeve. With that, she dabbed her face, collecting the tears and deep regrets that lingered there. "You have responded to all this with helpfulness and acts of kindness. I feel so very much ashamed."

"Might not have spoke on it, Miz Coverdale," Cowboy said after a moment, "but I was reared in a God-fearing home. Each night after supper Ma or Pa would read us Scripture, to school us in those mindful ways."

She nodded with a knowing look. "There was an old Bible left in the cabin when we got there," Prudence said. "I have been reading it for some needed comfort. One of the Psalms says, 'I will lift up mine eyes unto the hills, from whence cometh my help. My help cometh from the Lord, which made heaven and earth.' My prayer was that such help be given us." She looked down at the hands in her lap. "Unfortunately, I was too blinded by my anger to consider that what *was* sent—was you."

He grinned with reassurance. "Lending a hand back there was the rightly thing to do."

"What about the money you put up at Kessler's store?" she asked. "I can't say when that ever will be repaid."

Cowboy held up a broad hand. "Truth is, I was gifted with that saddle by circumstance back up the trail. Fair to say it was heaven sent. Sharing that just makes my heart go easy." His ready smile made her heart feel lighter. "If what I done gets you and Isaac off to a fair start, then I'm paid-in-full. Texas can use good folks like you."

Prudence rose to her feet once more. She took the time to straighten out her dress and coat. The moistened kerchief got tucked back into the cuff. "I have trouble expressing gratitude. I must confess I don't know why that is."

"Well, ma'am," Cowboy said. "I'm told it starts when we realize that nothing in this world gets done by the strength of ourselves alone."

"Then, thank you for the gift of deer and cougar pelts. That covering will keep us warm at night and give us peaceful sleep. God bless you, 'lone *baccaro*'."

She squeezed his big hand with both of hers. A look of warmth and budding encouragement replaced the former desolation. Prudence let go with obvious reluctance, turned without further word, and left Cowboy standing alone in the dining room.

***

Fed, watered, and saddled, the big horse was ready. Cowboy looked again into the heavier of the two cartridge boxes he'd gotten from the preacher weeks before, along with the Sharps rifle. Four huge gold nuggets were all that he could see. "It's doubtful," he said to Dusty, "Brother Van knew that dead prospector found treasure in the mountains after all."

The wrangler shrugged. Finally, he accepted that this gift was meant to be his. "I reckon them pieces is enough to buy back Pa's ranch from that chintzy banker. Takes some of the sting out of going home." Cowboy heaved himself into the saddle. With the press of a single knee, he turned his mount south toward Atascosa.

They loped the trail at an easy pace.

Their journey had begun.

All That Glitters
Study Questions

1. How is Cowboy's generous gift of canceling the debt without seeking anything in return like God's gift of salvation to us?

2. Why was Cowboy willing to give so much? How did Cowboy knowing the saddle was not his make him willing to be generous?

3. We are all like Prudence, because we have a debt we cannot pay. How is that debt paid?

Any Horse in Texas

Big or small, a cattle outfit is only as good as the horses they ride. It matters not what time of year, the color, or the breed — or even whether you're standing north or south of the river. In Texas, there are only four cow pony temperaments to be found: the jumpy, the good-natured, the loner, or the all-but-unbroken. Cowboy knew this. He also knew that a man cannot teach a horse without being taught in return. The many miles he rode on Dusty begat their friendship. Countless days they spent together forged their trust.

Cowboy believed that with a good horse beneath him and a dependable rifle within reach, he could trek just about anywhere in cattle country to get work done for the brand. His big buckskin was no longer a colt, although Dusty had not been much older when Cowboy chanced to saddle him the first time. Now, the wrangler let this horse — still strong in his gait— lead the way down the trail, familiar or unknown.

For three days they followed the river south until horse and rider came to the old military highway. That worn dirt road extended west as far as El Paso, after crossing over the Pecos. To the east, it made its way to San Antonio. Cowboy turned Dusty now heading toward the Alamo city. At the horizon's edge, bumping up from constant flats that seemed only interrupted by occasional curly mesquite clusters and knots of buffalo grass, the wrangler saw the beginnings of the central hill country. "Dusty," he said, "best to start remembering where it was we last saw Emma. I calculate by sundown tomorrow we'll be close. And we got that promise to keep."

145

That recollection together with the mild air and bright sunshine brought the cowman much contentment. The mood stayed with him as they veered off the broad throughway to take a lesser road used by freighters and mail coaches to reach the small towns started there by hearty German immigrants. Cowboy recalled these Rhinelanders loved to haggle over every little thing. They deemed no detail insignificant.

The sun had yet to cross the noon meridian when they forded a narrow stream that barely reached Dusty's fetlocks at full depth. Beginning immediately on the opposite shore, an uphill grade began. Steep and more rocky than sand, the road held a tight band of shoulder-high vegetation near its crest. This dense Rabbit Thorn thicket clustered over an acre or more on both sides of their pathway.

As they made their way slowly almost to the top, Cowboy saw that a small clearing opened to his left. He doubted that gap could hold ten small cows or three large longhorns, but his eye was drawn to the commotion unfolding in its midst. By the agonizing cries, the horse sounded in serious pain. The gelding tried in vain to loosen the grip of the man standing on the ground beating him across the withers.

That distinct sound of leather striking flesh stirred Cowboy's anger. He wheeled the buckskin in that direction. Almost without urging, Dusty sprinted toward the bully at full gallop. As they approached, Cowboy could see the cruel assailant to be a young man of eighteen or nineteen years. His hat lay stomped on the ground. One suspender fallen off the shoulder now draped across his elbow.

Neither hearing nor seeing the encroaching horse and rider, the young man dropped the belt from his hand to pick a coiled lariat up from the ground. He seemed single-minded to continue the brutal flogging.

"STOP THAT, you crockhead!" Cowboy yelled, "You got no call to whip an animal like that!" He reined in Dusty with one hand as he leaned out over the saddle. The wrangler caught the rope's loop as it reached the top of its backward arc. He slid quickly to the ground still clinging the lariat. Without too much effort Cowboy won the brief tug-of-war, ending with his complete possession of the rope.

For his part the young man looked neither chastised nor concerned, let alone afraid. He spoke first, "I'ze you, old man, I'd get on my horse and ride away from things that ain't none your business." His eyes betrayed a mild amusement. His body crouched into a dare.

Cowboy calculated that he was not old enough to be this boy's father by any stretch, and second, that he'd seen this hot-headedness many times before. All too often, in those rough-and-tumble supply towns along the trail, some rider from another outfit would spoil loudly for a fight. The reason didn't really matter; neither did the victim.

"Well, I ain't you, *pendejo*," Cowboy said in quiet tones, "'Cuz I know that twenty miles in one direction and forty in the other with no town in sight, is not a place to be crippling my only means of getting there." The wrangler raised the rope buckle high. "Getting lashed with loops of braided hemp hurts like blazes." The lariat swayed slightly in his grip, inviting the shorter man to learn if what Cowboy said was true.

The youngster coughed out a high-pitched snort. "What *you* don't know," he said, "is that I'm Kid Tyson. I could air out your liver with this Schofield 44." His hands hovered over the darkened pistol butt in anticipation.

Cowboy brushed past him without a word, outstretching his arms with palms down, to ease up to the pinto pony now cowering against the juniper hedge. For minutes the wrangler took small steps, spoke gentle tones, and finally placed a hand on the pony's rump, halfway between back and tail. Once he felt the horse relax a bit, Cowboy ran the hand down one back leg and lifted up the hoof for an appraising look.

"See that dark color there? Around that small stone stuck in the groove between the frog and the sole?" Cowboy asked. "Got a bad bruise. He's road sore for sure." Disgust spread across the wrangler's mouth and eyes. His head shook back and forth in disbelief. "Sakes alive, *hombre*, didn't you feel him limping?"

Cowboy had to repeat his last question to get an answer. Rather than take interest in the pinto's condition, Tyson devoted most of his attention instead to the buckskin. He paid careful attention to the rigging, saddle bags, and rifles that the big horse carried.

"I thought he was just coming up lazy," Tyson said, "Cussed him for being so troublesome after we came though that rock field yonder." He nodded off to his left. Not a care seemed evident on his face. "Couldn't keep him to a trot much after that. But we still made good time and nobody saw me come up to this hidey place."

Cowboy approached the pinto once more. He touched the still sticky drying blood oozed from a series of short gashes across the flank near the belly. This damage came from the huge rowels of the boy's spurs, each containing fourteen sharp points. The wrangler turned back to the young rowdy once more. He said, "You call to mind an old pal I rode the cattle trail with many times. He was tough on his horses, but not merciless like you. Name of Frankie Peppers."

"Told you, old man. My name is Kid Tyson."

Cowboy ignored the protest to continue. "He was mixed-blood. His ma came from one of the northern tribes. She was the one taught him how her people view nature and the world."

Tyson eased slightly his posture from obvious provocation to a more mild interest. "What's this to do with my lame horse?" he asked.

"One night over bacon and beans," Cowboy said, "he told us how his ancestors believed that when they looked into the eyes of a horse, they did not just see an animal. Instead they saw another living being. They saw a friend. They felt its soul."

"Yeah, well, I'll tell you what I see." Tyson said, "four hooves, a mane, and a tail. One nag is as good as any another." He dropped down into the crouch again. This time, he drew the Schofield from its holster. That, he leveled at Cowboy's chest. "Me and this buckskin of yours are going to ride together from now on." His lips curled into a grin, that of a wolf about to snarl. "Seeings how both your rifles are strapped to this saddle and you carry no pistols in your belt, I expect you won't put up much fuss." Tyson laughed. "Call it an even trade for the pinto."

The wrangler stood unmoving. He looked first to Dusty, whose ears cocked forward as if he were following the words being spoken, then to Tyson who backed up far enough to grab the reins still draped in a ground tie. "Afore you go to getting in a bad way," Cowboy said, "I must apprise you." He raised one big hand to point directly at Dusty's head. Instead of using just the index finger, the hand extended as though forming a salute. "Dusty's not easy to sit saddle on. In fact, he has a streak of mean."

Undeterred, Tyson responded with a practiced casual boast, "Old man, it's a known fact that I can ride *any* horse in Texas." He threw one rein around the buckskin's neck. With the other in hand, he stuck his boot up at a stirrup. He missed twice as Dusty crabbed a step or two sideways each time he tried. Cussing now, Tyson grabbed the horn and, with seeming ease, swung himself atop the saddle in a single effort.

"Whatever you have in mind," Cowboy said, "one thing you should ought never do…"

The words came too late. Tyson jerked Dusty's head around with a ferocious tug. "I'll show you who's boss," he told the big horse. The rider sunk the spurs of both boots into Dusty's sides. That got the buckskin moving - but not as Tyson intended. From a restless standstill, Dusty bolted like a shot for three long strides. Horse and rider were soon to the opening of the thicket, only a few steps from the roadway. Without so much as a break in rhythm, the buckskin lengthened his gait ever so little. Then he jammed both front hooves into the dirt. His neck bent down so that the jaw now almost grazed the ground.

Unprepared for this unexpected drama and caught with his weight too far forward to recover from the sudden stop, Tyson barrel-rolled heels over hat to land hard on the rocky roadbed. His right shoulder took the brunt of the fall. He didn't bounce much, if at all.

Cowboy came at the run. He hoped to prevent what he feared was coming next, but he was not nearly quick enough.

Dusty reared up slightly; sufficient enough to bring his hooves down hard on the rider's body. Once. Twice. Three times the big horse did this before Cowboy could pull him away.

The wrangler eyeballed Tyson's chest until he could see him breathing. "God ain't through with you yet, pard," Cowboy told the prostrate figure covered in the trail's dirt and dust. "Otherwise you surely would not survive a fall like that." He saw the blood start to drip from the young man's mouth. "Tried to warn you that Dusty don't much cotton to spurs."

Cowboy waited in silence. For minutes, Tyson did not respond beyond taking shallow and increasingly noisy breaths. "You're busted up good," the wrangler said softly. "Can you move at all?"

At last the young rider stirred, rolling his head to one side. With what little wind he could muster, Tyson began to cough out phlegm, saliva, and blood. "It hurts all over. Mostly my shoulder and ribs." he said in halting whispers. He tested his left arm, to find it still useful. Tyson placed a hand on Cowboy's forearm, clutching it more as he found strength. In a voice now no more than a groan, barely to be heard above the afternoon's light breeze, Tyson said, "Please, mister, don't let me die out here alone."

He eyes closed as a stupor overtook him. The young rider left Cowboy alone with only the sounds of raspy wheezing.

***

Stopping for a moment, the wrangler watched dusk fade to encroaching darkness. In the southwest, the evening star dazzled like some bright beacon. Cowboy lamented that this early in the year, its stellar companion no longer paired up for their nightly celestial journey. That other star lay hidden now somewhere below the horizon.

Since Tyson spoke to him last and swooned, Cowboy busied himself with a host of needed tasks. He gently pulled the stone from the pinto's hoof. Then rubbed the wound with the juice of a single chili pepper found abandoned in the bottom of his saddle bag. Something he watched *vaqueros* do time and again on the long cattle drives north. It was said to reduce any swelling. This pony put up no fuss at all.

To give the injury an extra measure of protection, the wrangler wrapped the hoof with small strips cut from Tyson's bedroll blanket. Removing both saddles, Cowboy hobbled the horses outside the juniper hedge. There, they could graze their fill on a tall patch of greening weeds and other rough vegetation. Last, he built a fire to boil coffee. Something needed to wash down the salted venison he chewed with slow precision. Cowboy took the little leather-bound book from the range coat's pocket, leaned on one elbow near the fire, and mumbled the words aloud to more fully grasp their meaning.

From the roadway, Cowboy soon heard a moaning and the rustling of movement. He turned to find Tyson almost sitting. The bad right arm clutched to the chest at an odd angle. Labored breathing came steady but loud. Once the young rider tried to suck in a complete lungful of air. Even in the campfire's dim light Cowboy could see the pain that caused.

"We're gonna need to find you a sawbones, for sure," Cowboy said. "What little doctoring I done in this life was first time I pushed cattle up the trail. Helped the cook tend to drovers' discomfitures, mostly rope burns and other scrapes and bruises." He looked at the sagging heap of flesh and bones that had been a feisty adolescent mere hours before. "Cookie told cowhands busted up bad they had three choices: find a doctor, tend to it theirselves, or die." His face took on a look of encouragement. "Them last two ain't in the cards—yet."

He helped Tyson to his feet with great effort. After a dozen plodding steps he got the young man off of the road and out of more harm's way. Cowboy propped the now quiet young man against a saddle next to the fire. He offered up supper meat but Tyson just shook his head. The boy did take the tin of coffee extended to him. He cradled the cup against his chest below the chin, letting the warmth comfort him some.

Tyson spoke. "I heard you muttering there in the dark," he said. "What is that all about? You that lonesome out here in the wild?"

"Never," Cowboy replied in a quiet but even tone. He held up the small Bible for Tyson to see. "As long as I got the Good Book in my hand and the Lord in my heart, I never ride these trails alone. How about you?"

"I hurt too much to talk church with you. It smarts even to draw breath." Tyson grimaced as he did so. "Reckon the pain will ever quit?" he asked.

"Not likely anytime soon," Cowboy said. "Now stick out that tongue of yours. Loll it over this away." Tyson did so. "Now tuther." The boy did so again. With a keen eye the wrangler saw the dark red knot swelling on one side of the pinkish tissue. It still oozed a bit of blood. "Bit yourself when you hit the ground," Cowboy told him, "That likely accounts for the mouth bleed. Could have been bad otherwise." He cut a juniper sprig from the hedge using his long knife. That he handed to Tyson. "Chomp on this."

Gently the wrangler ran long fingers along the young man's ribs, stopping whenever Tyson flinched or moaned. For several minutes Cowboy repeated this crude examination until satisfied. At last he said, "Seems some is cracked, others is broke. None poking through. That's lucky," He nodded to the boy. "But you need help better than me."

Tyson spit green bits and resin from the tip of his tongue. He tried washing the bad taste out with the remaining Arbuckle coffee but bitterness lingered. "That hedge is no good for eating," he said.

"For a fact, it ain't," Cowboy replied, "but it's a good place to hide. What was you doin' hole up in the junipers? More than just beating a horse."

Tyson shifted from resting on one hip to the other. His eyes did not quite meet Cowboy's. "Guess it don't matter much now," he said. "I was fixing to rob the stagecoach on its way to Mecklenburg. Gonna steal their strongbox full of gold and silver." His eyes still lit up at the thought of it.

Cowboy could not help himself. He laughed from deep in the belly. "Well, Kid Tyson," he said, "How you come to figure on that? We're miles south of where the Oxbow Route carrying the Overland Stage crosses that military highway. Only gold around here gets hauled is by the U.S. Army. And that's on the big road back yonder." The wrangler shook his head in true disbelief. "Last I seen, that Army pay wagon always has a troop of armed cavalry with it." His arm stretched out to point at the dirt track he'd just taken Tyson off of. "That path is too small for a Comstock Coach like the Overland outfit uses." Cowboy said, "Most can travel this path is a farm wagon or that buckboard carrying mail under government contract." He shook his head again in amusement. "Doubtful you'll get rich bushwhacking either of them."

The wrangler stood, grabbing the remainder of Tyson's torn blanket. He began to rip a long strip from the remaining material. All the while Cowboy could see that the boy followed his movements with a mix of wonderment and scrutiny, but Tyson said nothing.

With the task finished and the knife back in the sheath, Cowboy rolled the remnant into a tight bunch. He knelt beside Tyson to place one end of the ripped blanket in the midst of the boy's chest.

"On a cattle drive once't out of Nueces," the wrangler said, "we had a cowhand not much older than you, get kicked by a longhorn bad enough to smash some ribs. Ray Patterson was the *segundo* of the outfit back then." Cowboy began to wrap the blanket under Tyson's arms and around his back. "Ray trussed that boy up tight with a length of canvas so the cowhand could breathe without hurting. It oughta work for you."

Minutes passed before the dressing cinched around Tyson's ribcage completely. The wrangler helped the boy stand so as to better judge the effect of his efforts. In a breathy tone, the boy said, "Tell old Ray for me that his cure has some promise. I can draw and exhale without so much hurt."

"Ray's dead," Cowboy replied, "but he woulda been the first to be happy for you. And the first to say you was stupid. A desperado you ain't." Cowboy tucked the tattered end piece under the bandaging. "What in the world possessed you to pick this very spot?" he asked.

Tyson's pride showed in the grin that gripped his face. "Easy enough," the boy said, "the road runs steep next to these junipers, coach is barely moving with all that weight. I get the drop on 'em sudden-like, relieve them of their strong box, and hightail it out of here a richer man."

"Come up with that all by yourself, did you?" Cowboy asked.

"Naw, it was that three-card monte scheme. The one where you bet some sucker that he can't follow the ace of spades when you shuffle just the ace, a ten, and a king on a table top. Like the game of thimblerig, hiding the pea under one of three thimbles." Tyson's grin faded to a face of clear regret. "Turns out I didn't have the hands for it. All thumbs. Ended up, I either lost money paying the suckers when they actually won, or got beat down hard when it was obvious I was trying to put the cheat on them."

"Sounds like you was the actual sucker," the wrangler said.

"Maybe," Tyson replied. He tugged the blanket strip with both hands to better fit his breathing. "Met this man playing billiards for money in a saloon near Kerrville. After three shots of red-eye, he blathered on about how easy it was to hold up a stage. Sheriffs covering too much territory, no money for posses, little interest in chasing robbers outside of their jurisdiction." Tyson eased himself next to the fire once more, taking up the coffee cup again. "He claimed he'd made a fortune robbing stages in California, but he must a spent it cause he sure looked down on his luck when I was there buying liquor for him and listening to him tell me his endless stories."

Cowboy sat opposite the boy, facing east. The darkness now began to fade to that bluish-black that foretells the coming light. He nodded toward hills on the horizon just beginning to be seen in vague silhouette. "Dawn is coming soon," he said. "I reckon you can still ride once we get you on the horse and if we go slow. With the pinto limping like he is, slow is all we got."

"And then what?" Tyson asked. An edginess crept into his voice; the sound of a man down in his boots, not that of defiance.

"I figure we back-trail to the military highway," Cowboy said. "Then head ourselves toward Austin. Long about Fredericksburg, we should come upon Fort Scott." The wrangler nodded to himself in the gathering light, agreeing with his own plan. "They should have a doctor there could help you out." He tossed remains of cold coffee on the fire's ashes, sending up a brief sizzle of thin smoke.

In a moment, Cowboy stood. He grabbed up his saddle and bridle leathers. "While I'm loading the horses, you should give some thought to changing your life. Keep heading down the trail you're on, and serious bad is bound to befall." He turned to go cinch up Dusty, but turned back when he heard Tyson's whimpering break out to a bawl.

"I'm just no good at anything," the boy said, "not bushwhacking. Not cards. I can't even rob folks with that big pistol of mine without ending up with more trouble than money." The boy wracked himself with blubbering sobs. The stabbing pain to his ribs lay hidden beneath the tears streaming over his cheek. "I'm a faker, too. No one calls me Kid Tyson but me," he confessed. "My real name is Burl Tyson. Baby sister called me Burley, before I run off from home last year. I was no good being a farm hand either. My father said as much." He looked up at the wrangler, eyes wet, confusion dancing there with the agony pouring from his heart. "What am I going to do?"

The wrangler looked down at the crestfallen young man. "You might begin by letting go," he said, "Stop clinging to the thoughts and deeds that bring you pain and ruin. Fall into the arms of the Lord and let him carry you to the destiny that He has planned for you." Cowboy stuck a hand in his range coat. At last, he pulled out the small Bible. That he handed to Tyson.

"You might want to look at the passage from Luke. Start with the twenty-third chapter, long about the forty-second verse. Just hours before he died, the thief on the cross called on the Savior. Even that man's soul was spared the eternal confines of Hell. I find great comfort in that."

Tyson did not take the book when offered to him. His look became even more forlorn. He said, "It's not that I don't appreciate your offer, mister. I can see you are a sincere man of God. It's not even that I truly believe the Lord would have no use for a low down fool like me." The boy swallowed hard without taking his eyes from those of the wrangler's. "Comes down to it, I can't read."

Heart almost breaking from hearing that knowledge, Cowboy squat on boot heels. He turned to the passage indicated and slowly read the Scripture aloud in his soft baritone. The wrangler looked up at each verse ending. Tyson nodded along as he heard each word being spoken. In the distance, the sunrise crested the meager treeless hills. Morning's first rays of light began to touch them both.

***

Tyson lay in the back of the Army wagon, resting on the contraption thrown together by the affable Sergeant Major McIntyre. Half hammock, half wounded man's litter, it swung freely hung by its ropes. McIntyre calculated the boy would rather sway a bit, than to feel each bump along the rock-strewn highway. He draped a stout cavalry blanket up to Tyson's midsection before stepping back down to his horse.

Cowboy shook the hand the Sergeant Major offered him. The Army man said, "It's more than a miracle that you found us out here on this open road. We only muster from the fort for supplies every fourth month." The man adjusted his uniform and tightened leather gauntlets to his wrists. "Your friend is in good hands now," he said, "and we'll see that he mends proper."

"I only come upon the boy a day ago," Cowboy said, "From what little we spoke, I'd say he has the makings to become a good man."

Mounting up, the Sergeant Major looked to Tyson first and then to the wrangler standing in the road next to his horse. "Army's short of volunteers at the moment," he said, "we might even try to recruit him."

McIntyre called orders to his troops, who responded sharply. To the wrangler he shouted over his shoulder, "We'll be late as it is. We must move out. Make your farewells, but please be brief."

Cowboy nodded. He approached the wagon's side leading Dusty by the reins. Tyson spoke first. "I've been figuring on this," he said. "Best thing could of happened was being tossed by that buckskin of yours." He slid his good hand out from the blanket. It surprised him that the big horse let him pet the tip of his nose. "Might never had that talk with you or heard that Scripture." He smiled. "Banged up as I am, I got time to think about my situation and what all needs to change."

Cowboy took Tyson's hand to shake. To him he said, "You can tell folks you're committed to follow the Word. You can say what you figure they expect to hear. You might even act in keeping with all that talk. For awhile anyway." He placed a big finger to his own chest. "Until the changes reach here, it means nothing. Remember, the Lord will always know your heart."

The slap of reins on horsehide jolted the caisson into motion. Cowboy watched the loaded wagon lumber down the roadway at a slow walk. Tyson's pinto had no trouble keeping apace. The wrangler mounted Dusty, turning him back toward the cut-off road to Mecklenburg. The buckskin's amble soon became a trot.

They loped the trail at an easy pace.

Their journey had begun.

Any Horse in Texas
Study Questions

1. Kid Tyson thought he was not good enough for God. What stories from the Bible can you think of where God loved people who did not deserve that love? Does anyone ever earn the love of God?

2. Can you think of people you've met who had a rough exterior to cover up hurts and pain from the past? How do you go about dealing with them?

3. Why was Cowboy kind to Kid Tyson after what Tyson had done to him? Would you have done the same? Why or why not?

Adam's Missing Rib

Boys hailing from Deep South states rode up the trail with more than just a love of grits, magnolia trees, and political passion. Their manner of speaking seemed both delightful to the ear and at times downright incomprehensible. The ordinary Texan riding beside them couldn't tell a scuppernong from pinto beans, or find a hushpuppy in a prairie dog town. Doubtful either he might locate Plum Nelly on a map.

But the Lone Star cowpunchers quickly understood what it was the Southerners meant by a blackberry winter. More than once a late season Georgia frost had shriveled all new growth of the not-yet-spring. Whole hillsides of blackberry buds withered there, wildly delaying that mid-summer sweet fruit. Texas was no different.

Cowboy wondered as he rode this part of the trail if the moderate last several days would continue to warm, or whether the hill country would be treated to one more morning's light freeze. That thought vanished completely as he rode Dusty across the small rise topped with the first Mexican Blue oaks he'd seen in months. The prickly pear patch huddled at their base was what the old *vaqueros* called *Lengua de Tigre*, the Tiger's Tongue. A narrow notch through the hillside allowed the railroad to pass through in a lazy curve. Beyond that, the northern edge of the Balcones Headland spread out below to reveal a small cluster of buildings that formed the growing village of Leesburg.

Well past its edge and in the midst of the open country, a substantial windmill turned a slow rotation. Each blade gleamed in the morning's sunlight; all eighteen of them. Cowboy guessed it took more than a hundred acres to hold the entirety of stout cow pens he saw standing there. Each enclosure brimmed with milling livestock. The continuous low murmur of congregated bovines, interrupted by random bellows, could not be mistaken even at this distance.

In the hour it took the wrangler to reach the stockyard, he marveled at the scope of operation John Calvin Quinn built in these last several months. Mulling that thought, Cowboy realized he did not know for sure just how long he'd actually been gone.

Cowboy reined Dusty in next to that first large pen in their path. It baffled him somewhat that the enclosure contained only short-horned cattle: Herefords mostly, with a scattering of Red Angus, and handful of Santa Gertrudis. Not a single broadhorn could be seen anywhere he looked. All of these beeves appeared to be yearlings.

To his left, Cowboy heard a wagon creak under heavy burden. Two short-necked Breton draft horses pulled the load with alternating strain and ease. The driver called out a single word to them, in a tone that sounded European. They stopped at once. *"Willkommen, mein herr,"* the man said. He continued in English once he saw this tall rider was, in fact, an *Amerikanisher.* "If you have come to buy the beef, we sell only to the meat houses up the railroad line." He pointed to the loading ramp next to the freight car on the tracks. The curved squeeze chute began to fill with hefty cattle, just now approaching the inclined steps and narrow deck. Four men strung along the fencing prodded the herd with wooden poles to keep them moving.

As Cowboy turned back from watching this maneuvering, the driver said, "If you're looking for work, we don't need men on horseback. Mr. Quinn wants the job done on foot and by wagon." He smiled with the satisfaction of knowing his employer would not have to deal with another Texas saddle tramp on the drift.

Cowboy acknowledged this information with a most thoughtful nod. He scanned the pens with a slow turn of his head. A dozen or so men hurried about performing various chores, two others on wagons, the rest afoot. "Where is Cal?" he asked. It delighted him that the driver flinched at his use of the boss's Christian name.

"He supervises the loadings today." Slapping the reins, the man all but huffed in farewell. Clearly he had wasted enough time in idle conversation. The waiting pair of chestnut-hued geldings leaned muscled chests into the leathers. A blow of air puffed from each large nostril. The wagon ambled forward as before.

Cowboy could feel the unmistakable sensation as the big buckskin began to tremble beneath the saddle. "I can smell it, too, Dusty," Cowboy said. The long familiar odor permeated his nose and sinus. It began a tangy dryness at the back of his throat. "Can't mistake the stench of this much cattle bunched together." The wrangler shook his head. "And not no dust this time to fill your nostrils for some relief. Close my eyes and I swear we're riding drag again behind some northbound herd."

The big horse paced anxiously, one step sideways followed two quick steps back. This signaled that Dusty, too, missed the rigors of pushing cattle across wide open prairie. For a moment they each clung to a bit of reverie before Cowboy turned his mount back toward the loading ramp.

Making his way past the now empty sorting pens, Cowboy watched the youngest man of Cal's outfit close each blocking gate behind the moving throng of beeves. Bumping one another and bawling loudly, they crowded down a narrowing walk way between substantial fences toward the chute. In groups of twenty or so, the cattle stumbled through the main gate opened ahead of them. Once inside this rounded corral Cowboy guessed to be the forcing pen, four men walked behind them swinging slowly shut the gate that squeezed them single file onto the ramp and then into the waiting railroad car.

Cowboy had never seen cattle loaded for transport before. At the end of the drives, he and most of the other drovers had already headed home with money in their pockets by the time this got done. So, he watched the goings-on now with a keen mix of curiosity and fascination. He also wondered how cattle confined like this might act any different from those cattle out in the open.

They didn't. The wrangler spotted the trouble-maker two full minutes before that fat brockle-faced steer erupted into sheer panic.

Any drover worth a day's wages and a full meal knows that, with such wide-set eyes poised on the sides of its skull, a cow can instantly view almost everything except what's directly behind. So when they repeatedly turn their heads back one way, then the other, then behind them again—it means they're nigh to being spooked. While the basic instinct is to follow other cattle in the herd, their greater instinct is survival. That means escape. The merest opening will do. Where no exit avails itself, frenzied bedlam soon follows.

Cattle all have good memories. The stirred up brockle-face couldn't recall ever being in this part of the pens before, only adding to his overall agitation. He stood immobilized for a moment while considering his uncertain situation. That's when mistakes were made. The youngest man in the work crew proved himself to be a flat-heeled cattle man at best. He took it upon himself to move the frozen steer along with a simultaneous shout, "get on, there," and the stiff whacking of the rump with a cane.

The boy might as well have fired a loaded artillery piece. The brockle-face rocketed some twenty feet toward the Hereford squeezed against the fence. Short but wide, she bawled when the steer vaulted across her hips with all four of his hooves. In another instant, the brockle-face managed to leap clear of the enclosure, scraping a big belly on the wooden top rail and making a wobbly landing in soft dirt. Seeing nothing between himself and those distant hilltops, the steer bolted in that far off direction.

Cowboy ignored the shouting and cussing that came from inside the pens. Twelve men racing on foot carrying only canes and long hickory staves likely would be no help. By his own instinct, Dusty jerked into action before the steer's first hoof hit the ground. At a dead gallop, Cowboy untied his lariat from the saddle. He used the rhythm of the buckskin's hoof beats to shake out a sizeable loop.

The escaping steer thrashed loudly through knee-high grass and vegetation bordering the feedlot. He did not hear the approach of horse and rider. His first indication being the rope tightening around his neck when it began to cut off his breathing. It took only minutes for Cowboy to lead the reluctant stray back through the nearest opened gate into an empty pen.

Cowboy feared that any man among the crew might become the object of the steer's unvented animosity. With a light tug of both reins, he backed Dusty into taking slack from the rope. The wrangler dropped to the ground, stepped to the brockle-face in three strides, and with a hand on each horn wrestled the somewhat confused bovine to the ground with an easy move. Cowboy simply said, "Now," and Dusty slackened the rope enough for the wrangler to slip it off the steer's head.

The gate opened to find John Calvin Quinn standing there: university educated, builder of the largest feedlot in Texas, heir to a sizeable railroad fortune, and a handsome yet down-to-earth man. Outfitted now in manure-covered boots, a dirt stained shirt, and rumpled canvas pants, he labored happily as a man of the workaday cattle world. "I knew that had to be *you*," he said to Cowboy, "the big hat, the buckskin horse, the thick moustache." He laughed in true merriment as he shut the gate behind exiting horse and rider. They shook hands with a grip that at once held warmth and the recognition of time passed since the last such occasion. "I swear, if it's not you wrestling down one of my horses, then it's you roping one of my fleeing cattle. Thank you for that." He slapped the wrangler on the shoulder. His grin almost touched both ears.

With a shout and a wave of the arm, Cal gathered the men around him. "Boys," he said to the gathering, "I'd like you to meet the fella that saved my life that misbegotten day I rode a loco'd horse into a clamorous town." The men nodded in various degrees of approval. "But more than just that," Cal continued, "this is the man who introduced me to Emma, and convinced me to hire her as my clerk." That brought a general whoop of appreciation and loud applause all around."

Cowboy realized that these men adored her the same as he did. Being taller than most, the wrangler could easily scan the entirety of the pens and buildings. He did not spot the named young lady any place about.

Cal noticed Cowboy's efforts. He offered, "Why don't you and I take a walk over to the office. I believe there is someone there who would very much like to see you." They ambled together in a comfortable stride, and in even easier conversation. Dusty trailed a few steps behind.

Ten yards from the building's porch both men halted when a door flew open without warning. A slender, auburn-haired figure stepped out, one hand touching the door frame. The loud gasp was immediate. "It *is* you!" she shrieked. In the few seconds it took to run the distance to where the two men stood, Emma became a fevered blur of flapping pigtail, pumping elbows, and a flurry of boots and jeans.

The excited impact of her head and shoulders slamming his chest almost bowled Cowboy over. Even though braced, he still needed a quick step behind him to maintain balance.

"You came back," she cried, "you really came back." Emma repeated those words over and again between sobs. Her muted tones emanated from somewhere buried around his midsection. For a long minute they stood this way: Emma crying hot tears of complete joy, Cowboy's arms cradling her warmly, and Cal watching them both with a growing fondness.

At last, Emma stood back a step to take an admiring look at her long-absent friend. She held both of his big hands in her much smaller ones.

Cal quit his big grin long enough to speak first. "If I were more of a jealous man, sir," he told Cowboy with obvious good cheer, "I would demand that you take your hands off my wife."

***

The mouse faces south. He stays a creature of clutter, but labors unceasingly to pursue order. The eagle flies east. From lofty heights he sees all. He was granted the gift of vision. The buffalo paws dirt in the north. His ample size suggests true abundance of those manifesting resolute action. The bear lumbers west. He seeks hibernation. His reclusive sleep reinvigorates him through peace and solitude. So the campfire storytellers told the other drovers about the circle of life.

Cowboy wondered why he recalled that yarn just now. For the better part of the last hour, he busied himself shoveling dried manure off the wagon onto freshly plowed ground. When he saw Emma smile at him from across the field he knew. The wrangler first met Emma in her uncle's big barn. At the time, he was shoveling manure into a wagon off of the dirt floor. His life, in this instance, had come full circle.

She walked up to the wagon. A wide apron was tied to her waist. She held the bottom corner of the cloth in each hand. In the deep pouch formed there, a full pile of potatoes cut to chunks jostled with each step. "Well," she said, "it's really not that much, but it was all I could find." With that announcement made, Emma dropped the load beside the wagon wheel.

"In the three days I been here, "Cowboy said, "you and Cal provided good company and fed me like a prince. Doing chores for the likes of you two is downright pleasurable. But I can't say as I become much of a farmer." He swept his hand to indicate her patch of turned earth in the midst of the nearby rolling tallgrass. "I expect as how you ain't got enough spud bits there to plant this entire acre."

"There you go funning me again," Emma laughed with lilting tones. "You remember Mrs. Hagebak? I roomed in her boarding house when I first got here." She looked at Cowboy as though he were a favorite yard dog come to get his ears scratched. "We became good friends. She got her nephew to plow a small plot for me as a favor." She laughed at the recollection. "I promised him a little money for his help, and shared with him that someday I'd have a huge garden. I came out here the next day to find he'd done all of this."

Cowboy nodded. In his mind he could watch that all play out. He tossed out the last of the wagon's load, jumping down beside the girl. "Where's Cal?" he asked. "Don't he get to help out, too?"

"No," she said. "He offered to. More than once, in fact. He did again this morning." Her face took on a look Cowboy had never seen before. Determination dissolved into an easy serenity. "Ever since I saw the garden that widow left my aunt and uncle when she sold them her husband's house near Cowtown, I wanted to learn how to work it." She looked in his eyes for a moment, knowing his connection to that old place. "Aunt Lydia kept me too busy doing my chores and all her work as well" I never did more than watch the weeds grow in that little spot by the barn." Her eyes lit up once more. "This will be my first real garden, so I wanted to start out small. And I wanted to do it by myself."

Cowboy removed a slender hickory stave from beneath the wagon's seat. He found a pile of them back at the feed lot. Using the knife from the back of his belt, the wrangler whittled a point to one end. If not exactly sharp, at least it became less dull. "How's it figure then," he asked, "that you got me out here with you?"

"Oh, I've always heard tell that cowboys are special," Emma teased. "I don't know about all that, but I know that you are." She placed her hand lightly on his elbow. "I wanted to spend some time today without having to share you. You'll be headed south soon enough."

The wrangler looked at the tip of the stave, seeing some final adjustment had to be made. He said, "And you reckon it wouldn't hurt none either if you was to work me some while you was at it."

"Well, there is that." She laughed at his suspicion. "What exactly are you're doing with that knife and stick?"

Cowboy shook the hickory in his hand. "Around here, y'all call this a cattle prod," Cowboy answered. "I intend to use it to keep from burying all those potato seeds in the dirt on my hands and knees." He picked up a potato piece to demonstrate. Grabbing the stave high on the shaft with point down, Cowboy hefted his hand to shoulder height. He rammed the point into the dirt, creating a hole deep enough for proper planting. Next he dropped in the potato, kicking soil back into the hole with the toe of his boot. "Just like Ma taught me when I was a kid," he said.

For the next two hours those steps were repeated: Emma would drop a potato eye where she wanted it planted. Cowboy would poke a hole next to it, nudge the potato in, and tamp dirt on top of it. They would stop only when Emma needed to get more bits from the pile near the wagon. They continued until all potatoes were buried.

Watching her walk back with that final load, Cowboy studied changes to the young woman he left behind those many months ago. Her hair still hung in a single braid tied with ribbon. It swept across one shoulder and tucked into the apron top. Now, Emma's face held a particular glow; almost a radiance. Her eyes nearly sparkled whenever she looked at him. More curious to Cowboy, a greater fullness had come to her cheeks and a bit more to her hips. Tanned skin gave off a certain healthy look.

"Mi *bonita*," he said, "I would say you been mostly happy since you come to Leesville."

"*Bonita*?" she asked half-mocking. "I thought your name for me was *mi chica*." Her bright eyes began to focus somewhere in the distance. "But you are right, life got so much better since leaving Cowtown and moving here. I actually work harder, but it seems like nothing at all." Emma turned to face him once more. "And I met Cal," she said, letting the notion stand by itself. "I will always be thankful that you made that happen."

Before Cowboy could plead any denial, Emma shushed him with a wave of her hand. She picked up the small basket from her side of the wagon seat. It held a thick bundle inside a red-and-white checkered cloth. This she handed to Cowboy for him to hold while she spread a blanket at the edge of the plowed ground.

Emma sat on the cloth while Cowboy squatted on boot heels next to her. He took the pastry from her proffered hand, but did not recognize it at first glance. "Never seen one of these," he said. "If'n it's you who made it, I'll bet it's good." The wrangler took a long whiff of the concoction. He could smell the traces of cinnamon cooked in butter. It's rumpled crust felt soft in his fingers. At the first bite, Cowboy could taste the fruit.

"Boy howdy," he said through a mouth mostly full, "that is somethin'." A hard swallow followed. "How's it called?"

Emma beamed at the surprised but satisfied look on his face. "Mrs. Hagebak taught me," the young woman said. "She called it a skillet cake." Taking a tentative nibble, Emma said, "This one is made with pieces of dried apple." She offered up a second piece which he took without hesitation.

"You feed Cal like this?" Cowboy asked. "Not regular I reckon. He don't look none too fat." The wrangler wiped crumbs from the big mustache with the back of his knuckles. "How long is it since you got hitched?"

"Oh, it's been four months now," she replied.

"Well, shoot-fire!" he said. "I been gone that long?"

"Yes," Emma said evenly. "It's been a tad more than seven months since you rode north. Cal and I worked together every day after that getting it all organized, men hired, and materials delivered to site." Her air took on a matter-of-factness. "One noonday while I was eating dinner in the back of an empty buckboard, he found me reading from the Bible you gave me." She smiled remembering. "That started long conversations about Scripture. We grew closer every day after that. Two months later he proposed to me in the parlor of the boarding house."

"And then," Cowboy said, "y'all found a preacher and said vows."

"No," she said. "The next week his father came to Leesburg to inspect the feedlot operation. Being a railroad man rich as Croesus, I expected him to look down on our engagement." She smiled with a new found pride. "Not only was he accepting, he was welcoming. A man of God himself. He insisted we come to Chicago so I could meet the rest of Cal's family." She then gushed, "We even took our honeymoon in this big hotel by the Great Lake. It was like a fairytale."

Cowboy placed a hand on her shoulder. He squeezed gently. "I'm proud for you, Emma. Plain proud." He held the touch for long seconds. "Sounds like you got yourself a good man, and that your matrimony has turned life to the better." He chuckled to himself. Or thought he did, but she caught him.

"What's humorous about that?" she asked.

"You just didn't look like a gal dragging her rope when I left here, is all. Didn't figure marriage for you so soon."

"So soon?" She blurted those words at him. "I turned nineteen while you were gone. High time for a woman to settle in." Her eyes focused keenly on his. "I was lead to this man by Providence. Something that I could not, nor would not ignore." She drew a defiant breath. "And what about you?"

"Me?" He answered in true perplexity.

She said, "You're not a spring foal any more, and it would break my heart if I thought you were just to drift about the rest of your days." Moisture began to well at the corner of each eye.

"Don't worry, *mi chica*," Cowboy reassured her. "A year ago, likely I woulda busted out at your remark." He stood up to full height, and extended a hand to her. With almost no effort the wrangler raised Emma off the blanket. "Thing is, I barely have eight years on you. Still young enough for a good woman to find worth courting." His face eased into a sober reflection. "Spending that day hiding in the cave with a bear trying to eat me has made me think on what I should do in this life. Settling down is a particular notion I intend to take up one day."

He folded the blanket, and placed it next to the basket on the wagon seat. "Wedlock," he said, "seems to do well by you and Cal. It gives me encouragement."

"Remember," Emma said, "In the Book of Genesis it was God who said 'It is not good for the man to be alone.' That was the first thing in Creation He said was not good. So God made woman to be Adam's companion and helper."

At her straightforward use of Scripture, Cowboy flashed a prideful smile. He pleasantly acknowledged, "As I recall Adam had to give up a rib in that bargain." His impish facade gave away his intent.

"Now you're just joshing me," she said. "It's not that Adam's rib just went missing. More like a marriage partner was found for him." Her smile matched his good humor. "You'd give up a little flesh and bone for a good wife, would you not?"

"Reckon that story gets told when I meet her," Cowboy said. "Afore that happens, I got to get right with the family back home. Done 'em a bad turn years back. *Corazón contrito*, a contrite heart and some *grande* restitution is what's called for."

He threw the remaining gardening gear in the back of the wagon. In a moment more, he helped Emma into her seat, took his, and slapped the horses into a fast walk. The wrangler turned when he felt her staring at him. She said, "You came back like you said you would. You kept your promise." It made her feel good just to say those words. "When you come back this way again it will be without such obligation." Emma leaned into him a bit without waiting for the road to jostle them together. "Know that you will always be welcome." She whispered barely above the creaking wagon sounds, but Cowboy already felt the warmth of her words down in his soul.

They rode home in happy silence.

***

"The only way to the mountaintop begins with a first step up that hill." With those words, Cowboy's Pa would extol his boys to a greater effort whenever their stamina began to flag. The wrangler knew that his Pa would never judge this modest knoll rising from the otherwise flat land to be a true mountain. Just the same, standing in front of the newly constructed clapboard house, it afforded Cowboy a pleasant view of the feedlot slightly less than two miles distant. The garden stretched out behind them over a slight decline.

Cal stood next to Cowboy as the wrangler tied bedroll and saddle bags on Dusty. Emma continuously came back and forth from the building's open doorway. With each trip she brought more essentials for the tall rider to carry with him down the trail. Foodstuffs mostly, but also a newly cut wind-rag with her fancy stitching on all sides, and a passel of handwritten notes Emma had composed to Cowboy in his absence. She had no clue where to send them in his absence; an old hatbox held them until his return. Emma asked him to only read those posts whenever he stopped to build a campfire at day's end.

"Whatever else could she possibly load Dusty down with?" Cowboy asked his friend. "She brings much more, I will have to fill the saddle's seat and walk my buckskin back to Atascosa." Both men laughed. The horse turned his head to them. His look all but said that the buckskin found little humor in their talk, except that he, too, had grown fond of Emma. Dusty already smelled the bag of corn dodgers she brought on the last trip; his particular favorite.

"I must tell you," Cal began, "that I really love this woman." He looked up into the wrangler's watchful eyes. "Emma has been a true blessing in my life. Not only is she a steadfast and gentle companion, but this pretty little lady keeps me moving on the right road." He looked back at the door in anticipation. "And, I must confess, Emma has stopped me from doing some plain foolish things."

Cowboy raised a single eyebrow in reply.

Color touched cheek tops as Cal continued, "I was just about to buy the *only* pair of albino breeding mules in all of Texas when Emma came back into the office. Instead of just throwing the charlatan out, she surprised me by asking what else he had." Cal's hand pointed to the fenced opening of the barn. "For a dollar he sold us that: Cinnamon, her one-eyed pony." The tiny gray mare rubbed a shoulder back and forth against the wood.

"I swear," Cal said. "Some days Emma dotes on that animal almost more than she does me." He smiled with true affection. "Another reason just to take her in your arms and hug her."

His face turned serious now. "As I spoke on it last evening," Cal said, "I could use you here to help me run things." He hesitated awkwardly. "If south Texas holds nothing more for you, please come back." He gauged the wrangler's brief consideration of this proposal, sensing only a bit of relief at the offer but no commitment.

"Thank you, kindly," Cowboy returned. "I intend to make Atascosa my future. Whatever that might be."

"Then consider this," Cal continued. "You know cattle: good ones, tolerable ones, and in my business the ones to stay away from. Right now I have no buyer's agent in that part of the state. But the demand for beef back East has yet to slacken."

Cowboy laughed. "I would be stealing your money, Cal, if I was to ride around most days saying, 'Buy that one and that one, let that one that one go'." He let his gaze wander in the direction of the distant feed lot. "Any puncher with an ounce of savvy could do that, and at half the pay."

Emma stepped out on the porch with the last of her bundles. "Just give it some thought," Cal said, slapping the big man on the shoulder. "You can telegraph me here if you change your mind."

Cowboy took the bundle in one large hand, He could feel the warmth of fresh baked goods even through the thick cloth. "What is this, then?" he asked. "More sweet victuals I don't have to share with Cal?"

"They're called *Āebleskiver*," Emma said with a laugh. "It's how the Danish make their doughnuts in the old country. Sailors took them on long voyages, so these might last until you get home." Her eyes reminded the wrangler of his Ma's last look at him when he mounted up for that first cattle drive years ago. Her tears quickly followed. She grabbed Cal's arm to steady her, but could find no words.

Sensing this, Cal took charge. "Emma wants, we both want, you to come back this way for at a visit from time to time." The man removed the hat from his head. "Maybe at the end summer — or the fall at the latest," Cal waited for Emma to find her voice before continuing, "Say for certain you'll come back to see the three of us then."

Cowboy bobbed his head in agreement as the younger man spoke his piece. He stopped mid-nod to digest those last few words. "What three of you?" he asked in all sincere puzzlement.

Cal grinned then with unbridled enthusiasm. "Well, sir, Emma is with child. The baby will come by summertime." Emma blushed at that announcement, but smiled weakly just the same. Cal put his arm around her for as much assurance as affection.

"That is right fine news," the wrangler said. He removed his big hat this time. "I'd be proud to come see what the Lord has blessed you with. Nothing in this world could keep me from it."

He shook Cal's hand in congratulations, and waited for the bear hug he knew was coming. Emma embraced him much stronger than when he left months ago to ride north.

"One last thing before you go," Emma spoke in a voice just recovering its strength. "I bit my tongue up 'til now, but I cannot let you ride off until I know."

"What might that be?" Cowboy asked.

"Cal and I only refer to you as '*the* cowboy' or '*that* cowboy'," she said. "We don't even know your name. We're not supposed to ask that of a man out here, but please won't you tell me."

Cowboy smiled. Without hesitation, he told both of them.

"That's beautiful," Emma said. Upon reflection, she continued, "If it's a boy, we'll give him your first name. If it's a girl, we'll give her your middle name. That is, if you don't mind."

Cowboy stood mute just trying to find his breath again. Before he could utter anything, Cal chimed in. "An excellent idea," he exclaimed. "Say you agree."

At last Cowboy said, "I don't have the words, so a simple 'yes' will have to make do." More hugs and handshakes followed. Dusty watched the unfolding folderol with patient dark eyes.

At last, Cowboy stepped into the saddle. He swept the hat still in his hand along the horizon from the busy railroad, to full cow pens, to freshly plowed ground. "God bless your family, and all He helped you build."

Cowboy turned the buckskin south, looking back one last time before the ground sloped behind a tree-topped rise. He eased Dusty into a trot.

They loped the trail at an easy pace.

Their journey had begun.

Adam's Missing Rib
Study Questions

1. When the steer ran from the loading process, Cowboy and Dusty sprang to action, roping him and bringing him back to his rightful place. Cowboy also used his know-how to help make potato planting easier. What skills has God given you that you can use for the good of other people? What skills can you work on to make them better and more useful to serve others?

2. Emma and Cal's relationship began when Cal found Emma reading the Bible from Cowboy. How can relationships be based on Scripture? Are your closest relationships with other Christians who make your walk with Jesus closer? Why or why not?

3. Cowboy's journey, and particularly his time with the bear, made him think about his direction in life. Emma quotes Genesis to Cowboy about it not being good for a man to be alone. Is pursuing marriage the right decision for everyone? Why or why not? If you are married, are you giving up yourself each day for your spouse? What are some ways you can better serve your spouse?

4. Emma and Cal had love for each other that was not based on how each person behaved. How is the love that Emma and Cal have like the love Jesus has for us? Do you love people more based on what they do than on who they are? How can you show love that is more like Jesus' love?

Remember No More

Legends about wind captured Cowboy's interest like no other: the names for it, the power of it, and even causes for the absence of it. Didn't matter, he would listen to any and all accounts with rapt attention. From the vaqueros on the trail he learned that a man standing with his back to the wind could know with certainty that storms would only come from his left-hand side. Near the mountains along the Great Plains, people told him winter's eastbound winds were dubbed the *Snow Eaters*. Stories there told of mid-winter currents rushing down the slopes so balmy that four feet of snow melted in a single afternoon. One old-timer claimed he'd been driving a buckboard into town, his team barely keeping pace with that blustery warm wind. His pair of horses was running chest-deep in snow, but the wheels were already axle-deep in mud. And, the cow pulled behind the wagon kicked up only dust.

Fanciful yarn as that account seemed, Cowboy instead could only concentrate on a story he'd been told that one night by Isaac Coverdale. It bothered the wrangler greatly that he could not fathom why this recitation rolled over and again in the back of his mind, almost without ceasing. Before his death, Cousin Charlie shared a tale told around the Isle of Cuba. It spoke of how the doldrums, that almost complete lack of wind, caused sailors traveling there to name that part of the ocean the Horse Latitudes. By tradition, English sailors were given a month's wages days before setting out to sea. Most frittered that away on liquor and lewd behavior; this wastefulness termed "the dead horse" for reasons not fully explained by young Charlie. After thirty day's sail, most ships reached the Caribbean with its relative windless waters.

With little to do in this calm and also to celebrate their freedom from debt, sailors would weave together horse-figures made of straw. They delighted in beating them with a stick before throwing the remains overboard, bidding farewell to their financial burden. That sight Cowboy likely would never see, but he hoped one day to fully understand the meaning of this tale.

The wrangler stood from squatting on boot heels next to the base of the town's Axtell windmill. Watching sixteen slanted blades turned by a slow breeze to draw ground water had unexpectedly begun the wrangler's dreamy recollections. Now, Dusty finished drinking from the mill's water trough. Rather than saddle up to ride those last sixty miles toward Atascosa, Cowboy ambled toward Schulenburg's main street, leading the big horse by the reins. He calculated they faced two more campfires together before reaching the outskirts of home. His coffee tin barely held half a spoonful of stale ground beans.

Of greater concern to the wrangler, this small town held the last public bath and barber shop this side of the family's old ranch. Cowboy judged that if he needed to eat a large heap of crow in coming days, best to shake Texas from his boots and scalp before he did so. To reach the first of the two dozen or so mercantile buildings — all wood-constructed, one-story, and standing free of each other — Cowboy had to cross a somewhat wide expanse of well-trampled dirt. No signage indicated whether that tract belonged to any one man, but that probably didn't matter. Cowboy smiled as he remembered how very little land cost south of San Antonio.

He counted four wagons, each pulled by pairs of stout horses. The closest stood in front of a building marked "Outfitters". Another rested next to the squarish white-washed store with the block-lettered sign proclaiming: "W. M. Vinson Groceries". The third stood all but abandoned in the middle of the thoroughfare. And the last wagon had halted in front of a building whose sign lay in unreadable shadow.

A group of men gathered at one establishment's arched entry. Built entirely of limestone blocks, it sat squat and substantial on the corner. The rough, light-colored exterior seemed out of place this far from the Hill Country. It surprised Cowboy not the slightest that this housed the Merchant & Farmers Bank.

Horse and rider sauntered across the wide street, headed directly for the grocery at the far end. Cowboy expected to purchase more Arbuckle coffee, maybe a confection or two as a gift for the family, and be on his way in short order. Taking his time to enjoy the faint sunshine that poked through overcast skies, Cowboy felt the mild breeze brush his cheeks. Spring was coming.

Cowboy chanced to read that sign hidden before by shadow. The building belonged to a law office, the esquire's name painted in crisp black letters: "Riley Culpepper — Attorney at Law". The wrangler read the words aloud, in a voice now as unsteady as his disquieted spirit had become. The wrangler's entire body flashed an immediate sweat. Cowboy stood frozen in the middle of the street. He would have remained so for more long moments had Dusty not snorted at him with either impatience or questioning. His mount tugged at the reins, jostling Cowboy out of his near trance.

"By Josh and Joan, Dusty," he said to his horse, "I haven't spoke that name since I cussed the boy and busted his jaw." Cowboy looked at the buckskin and back to the sign. "If it be him," the wrangler continued. "But how many men in these parts could have that name?" Cowboy shook his head a long moment. "A lawyer makes money with his mouth — and a ten-gallon one at that. Trifle hard to do when it's all stove up bad like his was, last time I seen it."

The big man squinted at the space in the glass between the partially raised shade and the somewhat fancy cafe curtain covering the window's bottom half. Sunshine's glare across the pane prevented Cowboy from viewing the room behind. He swallowed hard once, and let out a long breath. At last the wrangler took the few steps to the post where he tied up Dusty.

After another moment, Cowboy crossed the wooden walkway only to find the door locked when he tried to turn the shiny embellished knob. Before he could let go of that brass, a man who'd been standing with the others in front of the limestones called out to him. "If you're looking for the lawyer," he said, "Culpepper's down at the bank. He always spends Wednesday at Merchants and Farmers."

To the man about to resume his walk down the street, Cowboy called back out, "How best to recognize him, mister? Don't know that I've ever laid eyes this fella."

"Easy enough," he replied. "Wears a striped gray vest, white shirt, and cattleman's black string tie."

Cowboy nodded his thanks. He slapped the buckskin's rump on his way past, headed to the bank. In the two minutes it took to cross the broken dirt street, the wrangler could find no words suitable to say if, in fact, *this* Riley Culpepper was his one-time nemesis.

The bank lobby proved as much a bulwark as the exterior seemed to be. A polished wooden facade took up one wall. Behind two black metal screens, clerks in suspenders and bowties helped townspeople with their money matters. Near a small barred window, a single desk and two wooden chairs nestled in the tiny remaining space. Sitting there, a man dressed as the stranger in the street suggested sat leafing through a stack of papers.

Cowboy studied the man, finding nothing familiar. The hair was too dark, the body too slender. When the man stood to reach a portfolio atop a nearby cabinet, he seemed too tall to be that chubby kid the wrangler remembered.

Turning back to his desk, the man noticed Cowboy standing there for the first time. The wrangler stared hard at him, not bothering to hide it at all. "May I help you, sir?" the man asked with practiced pleasantry. "Is this your first visit to our bank? Your first time in Schulenburg?"

When Cowboy heard him speak, in an instant he could recall listening to that voice in a hundred conversations, most of them harsh. To Riley he said, "You Strack Culpepper's boy, the one we all called *Pudge*?"

For a long and soundless second the man only blinked eyes in wonderment and curiosity. "Well saints alive," Culpepper laughed, "I haven't been called that in years. Used to be quite the fatso as a young'un." He now focused on Cowboy, but could not place this stranger from days since passed. "I don't recognize the mustache, or the hat. Maybe the eyes a little," he let that trail off, still trying to call this man to mind. Not until the wrangler stepped closer toward the desk did any memory flicker in Culpepper's head. "That walk," he said in a rush of breath. A budding recollection began to unsettle him. "The last time I saw a man walk like that, it ended in a severe whupping for me." It was Culpepper's turn to swallow hard. "Lord save us," he whispered. "You're little Johnny's big brother." The man went more pale than his starched white shirt. "You come here like you promised one day you would? You come back to finish that beating?" Silence filled the space between them.

***

When faced with fearsome threats to the tribe, the peace-loving native peoples of south central Texas knew that they could just take off running and hope for the best. Or else the tribe could stand and fight with those few weapons they had at hand. Instead, venerable elders of the Coahuiltecans [kwa WEEL teh kens] band, living on the banks of the San Antonio River, counseled a third option: strike a truce with the attackers and abide with the terms. Better to live in a forced friendship than lose blood on a knife's edge or die at the sharp end of a warrior's lance. But the Europeans marching north in search of gold posed a much different menace. The Conquistadors cared nothing for tribute payments of crops or livestock. Rather they wanted accommodating citizens for their new colonies. But neither the soldiers nor the Franciscan monks among their number spoke any of the seven Coahuiltecan dialects. Tribal leaders viewed these Spaniards with equal parts apprehension, wariness, and suspicion.

Cowboy calculated that was the same look he now saw on Riley Culpepper's face. The young attorney sat behind a polished oak desk in his law office, shelf upon shelf of imposing leather bound books stood stacked behind him. He listened as the wrangler finished telling a story of life on the trail.

"You'll have to give me a moment here," Culpepper said. He poured water from a hobnail glass pitcher into one of the four matching tumblers. This he handed to Cowboy before filling the second for himself. After two swallows, he set the glass down and said, "Did I hear you say that you rode out of Atascosa County never to return because you were afraid of *me*?" Culpepper pushed himself back more against the padded chair as though to

179

further distance himself from a rattlesnake he just discovered coiled in a corner.

"I was between hay and grass back then, a boy growing to a man," Cowboy said. "More fists than brains. The pure Simon truth of it, I figured busting a man's jaw like I did is like breaking a pony's leg. It ruins him for life." He shook his head with eyes screwed shut, remembering the shame he created. "A man can't eat, can't really talk; and the disfigurement lasts forever." The wrangler opened his eyes to face Culpepper once more. He struggled to square that harsh memory with what now sat before him.

A smile of untold relief spread across Culpepper's face. "As you can see," he said while running the fingers of his right hand along the jaw. "Even in this shadowed light, my face is just fine. Handsome even." Culpepper laughed at Cowboy's apparent discomfort as much as at his own half-playful attempt to buck himself up.

"But I broke it," Cowboy said. "I seen that when you was lying in the dirt trying to regain your senses."

Culpepper nodded. "I thought it was, too," he said. "I couldn't open my mouth, nor close it either. Hurt clear down to my shoulders." He put a palm flat against the jaw to test it one more time. "My folks took me to old Doc Crenshaw. After fussing around a bit, he told me to look at the ceiling. Then he stuck a big thumb under my tongue and grabbed my chin with those stubby fingers of his." Culpepper squinted as he thought of that night again. "He yanked hard. All I could see was stars in my eyes through falling tears. Before I could even take breath to scream, he yanked again. Harder. This time it sounded like someone snapped a dried pulley bone, but the jaw popped back into place. Out of joint, it seems. Not broke." He demonstrated this to Cowboy by flexing and closing his lower jaw. "Works just fine," he announced with guarded satisfaction.

"Your ma and pa must have been angry as hornets," Cowboy said, "When they seen it was me done this to you. My family owed money to your pa's bank for the ranch, and he never seemed a forgiving man."

A long silence hung between them for the second time that day as Riley Culpepper gathered the words he needed to say. "I never told my parents about the fight," he said finally, in a quiet almost matter-of-fact tone. "Pa thought I just fell off my horse again," he went on, "landing on my chin this time."

"What?!" Cowboy choked out in a whisper.

He stood up so fast that his now empty chair fell back on the plank floor behind him. In a moment more, his eyes grew to the size of Morgan dollars, but the look turned inward. It did not see the young lawyer with both hands now flat on the fancy oak.

"You mean," Cowboy said, halting between each incredulous word. "I didn't need to..." The import of Culpepper's words hit the wrangler like a mule's kick to the gut. It took breath away. He sat down hard on the chair he pained to upright.

When wits returned, Cowboy simply asked Culpepper, "Why not?" He could not fathom any reasonable explanation.

"If you recall," Culpepper said, "you kicked dirt on my chest with your boots as I lie there. When I refused to get back up, you told me, 'If you ain't learned the lesson yet, Pudge, I'll sure to come back and finish it." He smiled at Cowboy, estimating there would be no further fisticuffs. "So, it was me that was actually afraid of you." He chuckled at bit at the notion. "We both left that occasion with reason to avoid the other. Too bad it took all these years to put it behind us." His look turned a bit sober now. "We've put an end to it now, haven't we?"

"No," Cowboy said.

Firmness in his voice left no doubt it was not over for him. The big man stood to lean part way across the lawyer's desk. This startled Culpepper until he saw Cowboy stick out a big hand to shake. He noticed, too, the tears that welled up and rolled slowly from the wrangler's eyes.

"I owe you a sincere apology," Cowboy said, "for bustin' you up like that, and causing such pain as you had to endure. I beg you to forgive me that. And I beg you to forgive me leaving without saying a word or owning up to what I done." He shook his head at the thought of his own shortcomings. "I took the coward's way out that day. Got on a horse and rode away."

Riley Culpepper seized the outstretched hand firmly as he, too, stood. "No one could ever say it wasn't a fair fight," he said. "I started it with all that childish taunting. I even swung first." He grinned. "The whole thing might have turned out differently if I had actually hit you." Both men laughed heartily at that. "In my mind," Culpepper continued, "there is no need, but without hesitation I will tell you that you are forgiven."

***

Most Nez Perce warriors had spotted fever.

Not that sickness of the body, but the liking for a breed of horse with spotted skin and white rumps: the Appaloosa. These lean horses of the Wallowa Valley herd excelled at enduring long rides over rough terrain. The tribe prized them for the ability to jump barriers with relative ease. Yet every Nez Perce also knew of the horse's iron spirit. Any Appaloosa would grudgingly let a human ride its back, but only as long as it suited him.

Cowboy and Culpepper stood in front of the first gated stall. The big barn doors swung out onto the town's main street. An opening at the back gave way to a small corral behind the building. The motionless Appaloosa stud stared back at both men through shiny black eyes. The muscles beneath its tough hide all but quivered as the horse restrained its tremendous energy.

"I know for a fact," said Cowboy, "the U.S. Cavalry thought them Nez Perce up in Idaho was fierce fighters." He laughed as he turned to the lawyer. "A lieutenant once told me that's 'cuz by the time they got to the battle after struggling to ride those headstrong Appaloosa, the warriors was already mad as wet hens. They just took it out on the enemy."

"Is that really true?" Culpepper asked, doubtful tones creeping in his question. "Or, you just funnin' me?"

"Well," Cowboy said, "most wranglers wouldn't pick 'em out of a *remuda* for that day's ride, if another hoss was available."

The wrangler stuck out a hand toward the horse's lip. He wanted to see the teeth, but the Appaloosa pulled its head aside. It took neither a step sideways nor a step back. Instead, the Appaloosa stood its ground. The look all but dared Cowboy to try that again.

"Seems a mite contrary," Cowboy said after a moment's consideration. "Got a rodeo on your hands with that one. Gonna take a top hand to ride him, for sure." He eyed the stallion a few seconds more, then said, "I'd let him be." Riley Culpepper nodded his agreement.

Both men moved on to the next stall. A scruffy sorrel mare stood at the back end of the enclosure. Her ears lay back flat, head lowered slightly, moving slowly side to side. Sweat gleaned off the ewed-neck, taking on its somewhat reddish hue. "No good horse comes in a bad color," Cowboy said without breaking stride, "but that dampness makes her look as dark as her mood. I'd wager she's only green broke, and got ridden hard to take the fight out afore you come." Cowboy continued walking with an easy stride. Over his shoulder he called to Culpepper, "How much does this hombre owe you?" he asked, "'cause what we seen so far ain't no top horse." The lawyer smiled but said nothing in return.

Cowboy stopped so abruptly at the third stall that Culpepper, still eyeballing the mare, almost ran into him. "Well I'll be cussed," the wrangler said, taking the full measure of what he saw. "Not seen nuther of these since Hector was a pup." The wrangler pointed with a slight ballyhoo to the brawny horse in the small confines. When Cowboy saw that this meant nothing to the lawyer, he said, "I'm figuring this to be that Mustang-Morgan mix." Even that drew no recognition from Culpepper, so he continued in growing annoyance, "Like the horse named *Comanche*, the only living thing to survive the Little Big Horn." Cowboy gazed at the horse now with some intensity. "You don't see them much down this way, if it ain't pulling cavalry wagon." He nodded at the fenced rear doorway. "Let's take a look-see at him in the open."

While Culpepper unlatched the entry into the corral, Cowboy eased the stall's gate open. He stood to one side, awaiting which direction the Morgan would take, and how fast he'd go to get there. To the wrangler's satisfaction, the horse ambled at a leisurely walk to the open dirt of the paddock. Once there, he circled the enclosure twice with purposeful methodic steps. Had the two men not stepped into his path the horse might have continued that walk the remainder of the day.

"Take this leather," Cowboy said, directing Culpepper toward the stout animal. "Let's see how easy he takes to being haltered."

The wrangler smiled. "Remember: ask a mare, tell a gelding, and bargain with a stallion. You're halfway there, he's already had the knife."

The Morgan stood some inches less in height than Dusty, but made up that shortfall in girth. His barrel of a chest stretched a quarter again as wide as the buckskin. Built like a locomotive's steam engine, the horse was long and round. From breast to hindquarters, the mass of muscled flesh bespoke the powerhouse he must be.

The young lawyer approached with caution, but did so with a confidence that surprised Cowboy. Without fuss or struggle, he buckled the crown strap into place. In a moment more Culpepper adjusted the cheek piece to fit the Morgan's sturdy jaw line. Finally, the man turned back to the wrangler with a grin evidencing his satisfaction at both the choice of mount and his seeming rapport with the animal.

"Don't look like he's the kind to spit the bit." Cowboy said. "That's sure. Now let's see how he takes to having a rider." The wrangler stepped forward to give a helpful leg-up, but Culpepper waived him off.

"How can I claim to be Texan if I can't mount a horse by myself?" Culpepper said. With those words, he grabbed a handful of mane just above the withers, flexed knees, and launched himself into a leap. The lawyer landed in the thud of a tremendous belly flop across the Morgan's back. With a twist and a quick jerk, Culpepper threw a leg over the horse's wide hips. Then he pulled himself up to sit astride the animal.

Another grin danced its way across Culpepper's face when he realized the Morgan did not try to buck him off. He nudged both heels into flanks, and in return got the horse to resume its circuit of the corral. Cowboy walked along side for part of that way.

"Henceforth," the lawyer shouted with glee down to Cowboy, "I shall call him Hadrian. He certainly makes me feel like a Roman emperor sitting up here." The sight of it, and that proud announcement, made Cowboy recall his old saddle pal from England; the one they all called Professor. He, too, was given to unexpected theatrics. The wrangler watched horse and rider round the fence line twice more before Culpepper finally halted the newly named Hadrian and slid himself to the ground.

Brimming now with unfettered enthusiasm, the young lawyer strode next to Cowboy. Culpepper reached out with a thin hand to slap the wrangler across one shoulder. He said, "You and your family have been a source of unending inspiration for me. And today is just more proof of that." He indicated the Morgan now poised in a restful stance, eyeing both of them with an unhurried curiosity.

"I reckon I don't know the meaning of them words," Cowboy said. "How come you to say that?"

"It took a full six months or so for me to realize it," Culpepper said. "If I hadn't suffered the beating that day, likely I would have continued on as the person you so rightly described." He nodded to Cowboy in affirmation. "In fact, I was fat, and I was lazy. I pretended to be some local big shot, but I was only living in my father's shadow." He shoved his hands in pants pockets to level a steady gaze at Cowboy. "I've since believed that big right hand of yours crossing my chin just pointed it in the direction I should be going." Culpepper shrugged, and cocked his head slightly to one side. "After that, to the surprise of both my folks, I settled into a life of hard work. I learned the banking business up from clerk to board member. And seizing the opportunity when it happened, I read law with a retired judge in Austin."

Cowboy stared speechless. He tried more than once, but no words came. Culpepper swept his hands from hat to boots. "Everything you see here today," the young lawyer said, "began with me picking myself out of the dirt that day, after the fight ended."

The wrangler took this news like some drifter finding cake in place of grits on a breakfast plate. It perplexed him. He asked, "You spoke of my whole family. How's that?"

"You might not know of it," Culpepper said, "riding throughout the wilds as you did. Several years ago there was a substantial panic. Most of it back East, but we felt it here, too. Businesses failed, families ruined, banks in doubt." His brow furrowed at the sheer recollection of it. "Every man-jack citizen in Atascosa wanted money in hand, so as to feel safe. Obviously banks didn't have cash on hand to do that." He flashed a pleasant look; put a light hand on Cowboy's elbow. "Your father was one of the voices that cautioned folks not to be so foolish. Ruining the bank would not get their money back, he told them." Culpepper spoke now with tones of true appreciation. "Your father the preacher, and a few precious others, saved my family's bank."

Cowboy mustered an unconscious intensity without thinking. He stared off hard at nothing at all, not moving except for drawing breath. Seeing the big man in this state, Culpepper spoke out in calm tones, "Looks like you could use a hot meal and a good night's sleep. Let's put up ol' Hadrian here and head over to the café."

They did so.

Along the way, Culpepper said, "If you don't much dawdle on the trail betwixt here an Atascosa, you'll be at the home place by Saturday." He bent closer as his eyes foretold a secret bout to be shared. "That's your mother's birthday."

"How in blazes did you know that?" Cowboy shot back, coming out of his heretofore stunned silence.

"Oh, Marcus told me about a month ago," the young lawyer responded with all earnestness. "Your brothers and their wives will be there. You showing up for the occasion will just bless her heart."

"Wives?" Cowboy said as if stepping back into a sluggish dream. To his way of thinking, Marcus, Lucky, and Little Johnny were still mere boys. He doubted they'd grown an inch since he left.

"Why yes," Culpepper continued. "In fact, your youngest brother married Alice."

At this, Cowboy stopped short in the midst of the broken dirt street. He whirled on Culpepper, grabbing up a handful of the man's shirt along the forearm. "You mean," he said, "Johnny's hitched to your kid sister?"

"Yes," Culpepper said a second time. "That makes us almost like brothers-in-law." He chuckled in bemusement at the big man seeming so staggered to learn that life in Atascosa went on without his being there. After a few more paces towards the supper table, Culpepper said, "Not only did you return to find yourself forgiven, you find yourself welcome, and back in the bosom of family. For better or worse, that now includes me."

Cowboy looked down at the shorter Culpepper once again, budding acceptance and dawning relief in his heart. To Cowboy Culpepper said, "I attended Marcus's church in Uvalde one Sunday. He seemed to look right at me when he quoted the verse. Psalm 32: 'Blessed is the one whose transgressions are forgiven, whose sins are covered. Blessed is the one whose sin the Lord does not count against them, and in whose spirit there is no deceit.' I came right home and put it to memory."

They stepped onto the wooden walkway running the length of the café. Cowboy grabbed the door's knob, but stopped his turn midway. The wrangler turned to face a bemused Culpepper. The meaning of the afternoon's conversation with the young lawyer, his once sworn enemy, began finally to sink in. Cowboy looked deep into Culpepper's eyes. "So," the big man said, "Ma and Pa still own their ranch?"

Culpepper squinted in a most genuine perplexity. "That's right," he said. In a second more the lawyer added, "Mighty silly question. Why do you ask?"

***

In the minutes after dawning, Cowboy squat on boot heels next to a grove of mesquite at the edge of Schulenburg. A clump of bushes already beginning to bud lay huddled next to the trees' scaly trunks. The cowman watched a dozen yellow-eyed grackles plumed with pitch-black feathers scratch through the sparse vegetation. Ear-splitting cries filled the cool morning until a lead bird called the flock elsewhere. Cowboy mounted the buckskin when he saw Culpepper approach riding the docile beast now known as Hadrian.

"Mornin'," the lawyer said in most good cheer. "I came to wish you a fair and safe journey." He halted the stout gelding, almost touching Cowboy's mount. The men shook hands in silence for a long moment.

Cowboy spoke first. "I told Dusty just at first light," he said, "events of the day just past may have been a conjuring, or perhaps a dream. When I seen you ride up on that sizeable warhorse, I knew it to be for-a-fact actual." He took a broken red stone from the range coat's pocket. The wrangler had collected it off the canyon floor of the Talking Wall in Arapahoe country. This he held up for Culpepper to see.

"Near where this fell." he said, "I learned native warriors of the Plains tribes pray for great strength. Not to be superior to their brothers, but so that they can fight their fiercest enemy — themselves." Cowboy handed the rock to the young lawyer. "Take this as a keepsake to remember that." Cowboy's face eased from philosophical to sober. He said, "If yesterday was a rematch between us, I'm the one got whupped. Just the same, I take heart in the notion that I have to fight myself no longer." He grinned in quiet contentedness. "I was lead to you before reaching home. The work of Providence, no doubt. I am now a free man, and that feels good."

They shook once more. Before Cowboy could release the grip, Culpepper pulled him near, saying, "The gold you showed me last night: that's a second secret we shall both keep, just like the fight we never had. I'll get you better than a fair price and tell no one how you came by that money in your account. Deal?"

Cowboy nodded without word, recognizing the generosity of Culpepper's offer. The young lawyer finished with, "And I'll get that factory-made rig shipped home like you asked."

Cowboy turned the buckskin south towards the track leading to Atascosa. Dusty's walk became a trot.

They loped the trail at an easy pace.

Their journey *home* had begun.

Remember No More
Study Questions

1. Culpepper quickly forgave Cowboy when he asked forgiveness for the fight. Do you find it hard to forgive? How was Culpepper able to forgive so easily?

2. Culpepper's explanation of how the fight changed the direction of his life made Cowboy speechless. Tell a story about a time something bad happened to you that God used for good in your life.

3. Cowboy decided to fight himself no longer after talking with Culpepper. What fights have you had with yourself? How can you make your heart like the Morgan, under your control, instead of like the Appaloosa, that fights back constantly?

Nonesuch

All manner of south Texas predators, those who feed only in darkness, had long since fled to their dens. Even the many night birds gave up trilling and warbling as the blackened skies along the horizon's eastern flat began to purple, then to gray. Only the relentless mockingbird continued unending crying, still seeking to protect its territory or to seek a mate. When the dawn did come, it would be to Cowboy's back as he sat legs folded on matted earth next to a slender scrub oak. Behind him his buckskin foraged sprouts and other succulent new growth near the scaly tree's tangled roots.

In the slow-coming first light, a solitary barn cat, returning from the night's hunt, crossed open land stretched out before the wrangler. His crossing did not go unnoticed by either Cowboy or by that ever vigilant feathered mocker. With cries of warning, threat, and self-righteous anger, the slender bird swooped down to barrage the tom time and time again.

Cowboy watched this gathering fuss with rising interest. It mattered not to the tiny attacker that his moving target was multiple times his size. Nor did it move him that such hungry cats kill rodents and vermin with equal ease—and even those few birds that stupidly chance to fly within reach. After the fourth such shrieking onrush, the done in barn cat went hotfoot to the safety of the wooden structures Cowboy could see across the way.

"A'tween you and me, Dusty," Cowboy said, "that mock-a-bird don't fear nothin'. Don't back down none when he thinks he's right." The bird landed on the branch of a nearby, but smaller oak. His victory song continued non-stop for most of the next hour. During most of that while the wrangler managed a half-smile,

191

remembering. In a whisper he said, "Pa always told us boys, 'courage is the hardest of the virtues.'" At that moment the wrangler wished he had more of it.

Cowboy soon watched the silhouette of a man move between house and barn. Whether relative or hired hand, he could not tell. Some minutes later, faint streaks of fluttering light began to dance along the one barn wall Cowboy could see through an open doorway. As it brightened, the big man knew a blacksmith's fire had been stoked.

Blowing to his face head-on, the light breeze carried the scent of budding mesquite and that of Acacia flowers. It brought with it the distinct sound of metal striking metal: irregular, varied strength of impact, and to Cowboy vaguely unsettling. The deep resonance of the clamor indicated that whatever object being struck was sizeable indeed.

When sun's rays first touched the topmost flange of blackened stove pipe, Cowboy saw a steady puff of smoke, the breakfast fire. At this distance, he imagined more than smelled the acrid char of wood. His stomach growled a bit as he recalled johnnycakes, eggs, and bacon his Ma would cook up most mornings. Sundays, birthdays, and special occasions saw the making of her specialty when she would happily announce, "Everything's better with biscuits."

Tempted as he now felt for a familiar hot meal to start this day, Cowboy chewed instead on bits of salted venison. He wanted to see more of the ranch's activity before bursting into their midst as either a surprise or dread. The wrangler did not recognize the tall contraption next to the old well. Its wooden beams stood clouded still in vague shadow. Where he sat under the oak, it favored a hangman's gallows.

From the under the porch on the side nearest the barn, two women emerged. The younger, her seeming red-brown hair swept into a bun, stood barely an inch or so taller than the other. A flowing gray apron covered the girl's plain farm dress. She carried a three-legged wooden stool upside down in one hand. The older woman, without mistake, Cowboy recognized as his Ma. The hair more gray, her walk now the slightest bit stiff, but the particular manner with which this wiry woman lugged the two-handled Stanley milk pail marked it definitely as her.

Cowboy drew breath at her familiar sight. The wrangler clenched one big hand around the oak's bark, tightening into a hard squeeze. That pounding in his chest he knew to be his heart, but it felt more like being walloped with a stout walking stick. He screwed eyes shut when they began to dampen, obscuring the woman from his vision for a long, long moment.

Next to the barn, a red roan mare and a gelding bay milled in the corral. Ears cocked on both as individually each one spotted the buckskin new to their grazing ground. In turn, they whinnied their greeting.

Hearing this overture, Dusty blew first through both nostrils then nickered back his loud reply.

At that sound, Cowboy's mother turned until her scrutiny beheld the lone figure and his mount together in the patch of oaks. She peered, but could not distinguish the man's identity. Ma said to the girl, "Would you just look at that." She nodded in the direction of the trees. "Must be the third drifter this month looking for some handout. He'll gladly settle for a hot meal." She turned back. "At least this one looks to take good care of his horse. We'll feed him after chores." With that, the two women continued on to the barn.

Cowboy began to heave himself off the ground. "Dusty," he said in wistful tones, "recon I'll walk beside you over to the homeplace. Give them more time to see us coming, so as to better judge peaceful intent." The wrangler, instead, remained seated when he saw the man open the corral gate with saddle and bridle in hand. Even in the strengthened light, Cowboy was yet to say who he might be. But from the dispatch and ease with which he set and cinched the leathers on the bay, the man seemed no stranger to horses. He mounted, came through, and closed the corral gate in less time than Cowboy would have figured.

Still cross-legged under the oak, the big man watched the steady canter as approaching horse and rider closed the gap to his location. At a distance of about some fifty yards out, Cowboy smiled. He knew only one person to sit saddle in that particular manner. Neither did most men ride holding both reins by the left hand. When the horse got reined in, Cowboy stood.

Still seated on the gelding, the rider called out, "Reckon you're passing through. Where you hail from?"

"*No legos de aquí*," Cowboy said in a deliberate flat tone. "Not far from here." He looked the other up and down. The face rounded more with maturity, no longer adolescent. The cleft in the chin, however, stayed the same. It took all the wrangler had not to bust into a wild fandango.

The man looked at Cowboy in turn for a long minute before fixing his attention on the buckskin. "That's a nice animal you ride, stranger." He nodded toward Dusty. "I guess you'll be wanting some grub before you head on your way."

Cowboy waited until their gaze met. Befuddlement that always comes before clear recognition flickered in the rider's eyes. To help the man out, the wrangler took a step closer toward the bay and removed the weathered Stetson. He stood so the man could see his full face in the sun. To him Cowboy said, "Older, taller, not so painfully thin. Still a good rider, and the first out of bed in the mornings. You always could talk the hinges off a gate. Ain't that right, Lucky?" Then Cowboy grinned.

Staring down into to the yet recognized tanned countenance, Lucky felt a shiver pass through his body. "Never seen that moustache before," he said. He looked deep into the wrangler's blue-grey eyes to be certain, swallowed once, and let go a breath. "Praise the Lord," he whispered. "*It is you!*"

***

From the very leaving of the oak patch, and without stopping for most of that short jaunt to the barn; Lucky all but crammed nine missing years of conversation into the length of the ride. His jabber answered some questions Cowboy held of family goings-on during his absence. Once inside the corral, Lucky stopped his bay alongside the buckskin. Seemingly now he drew only the second breath since recognizing his brother a half hour before.

"Ma is just going to jump over the moon," Lucky said. "She has waited for this day ever since you rode off on that skinny pinto."

He grinned like a tinhorn holding aces in a game of draw. "You better have a darn good excuse to tell her, big brother," he said. "Deep in her heart she thought you was dead. But another part of her held out some meager hope." He leaned in close to Cowboy. "Every night, including this last one, she goes out on the porch. Don't matter the weather. She faces north, the direction she last saw you heading, and says a prayer." That news sobered Cowboy more than all that Riley Culpepper had told him.

The two dismounted. Without a word, they had removed tack and bridles from their mounts, freeing the horses to the expanse of the mesquite enclosure. Cowboy slid blanket and leathers over the split top rail of the fence, binding it securely. He angled back towards Lucky. "Let me put this off no longer," he said, drawing a deep breath. "I need to begin to make amends to her."

Both men stopped about three paces inside the barn. Behind them sunshine poured through the open large doorway, flooding the dirt floor and surroundings with unfiltered morning's light. In the stall centered on the far wall, a brown Durham cow chewed a jaw full of hay while the women tended to its milk-gorged udder. The younger, seated on the stool, slid a wooden bucket to the other. It brimmed with warm off-white liquid. Ma bent over the metal pale, her back to the doorway, ever so slowly draining raw milk into the dented container.

The younger woman noticed the pair of men as they stood motionless within an arm's length of where she sat. She stared at the stranger first, then at Lucky. His broad lopsided grin seemed out of place in the midst of restless cows, feed hay, and milk maid chores. He stood some two inches shorter, and a bit more narrow in the shoulder than the stranger, but shared the same sturdy cheekbones. "Is that..." she began before Lucky waved off the question by putting a single finger to his lips and a shake of his head.

"I fetched that drifter from the oak grove like you wanted," Lucky said. His eyes danced with laughter, confusing the girl even more.

Almost finished with her exacting task, his mother held her talk until the bucket emptied. "Good," she said, her back still to both of them. "Tell the man to wait and I'll cook him up enough to fill his belly."

Cowboy took two steps forward, removing his big hat for the second time that morning. The girl watched with eyes that grew larger as he approached. The big man said quietly, "Does that include some of your biscuits, Ma?" He braced himself to whatever came next.

For a moment nothing happened. Not a thing moved: not Ma, not the girl, not Lucky, nor Cowboy. Even the milk cow's constantly swishing tail stopped swatting at flies. With painful slowness Ma straightened from over the pail. The handle of the empty bucket held in one tiny hand, she turned toward the curious but not altogether unfamiliar voice. At first the sun's direct rays made her squint, standing as she had in comparative darkness. Cowboy took one step closer. His face alternated joy, pain, longing, and supplication in rapid order. His eyes locked onto hers. The milk bucket crashed to the dirt, rolling away slightly from her feet. Ma brought both hands to her mouth trying to cover the scream that came without warning. For such a slender woman, she filled the barn with ear-splitting noise.

Then she sobbed in more controlled tones, "My baby boy!" as Cowboy took her full in his arms. The two of them cried together for countless minutes. "As you always told us boys," he said, "there's nonesuch place as home."

Lucky grabbed his wife by the hand, lifting her off the milking stool. "Come on, Caroline, let's let them have the barn to themselves. They both need this." The two now-interlopers left quickly.

***

In the house's kitchen, Cowboy sat at the familiar long table. A filled coffee cup rested on it between his two big hands. He tried his best not to appear uncomfortable or lazy. Slow breathing helped. He had been instructed most lovingly by Ma to just sit where she could see him while she dealt with meal fixings.

The wrangler noticed his recently introduced sister-in-law peek up from the butter churn with every other stroke of the rod. Her hands rhythmically bumped the wooden splash guard on top.

The look spread across her face bespoke more of indecision than curiosity.

On the fourth such glance Cowboy said to her, "What about me are you trying to determine, Caroline?"

"It's not you, really," she said. "It's my husband, your little brother. His description of you is nothing how I see you now." She paused to restate it better. "I mean the way he said you looked when you left home." She stopped again, adding: "Back then."

"Oh," Cowboy replied. A smile began at both corners of his mouth. "And, how was that exactly?"

"He never let on that you had such good looks," she said. Caroline shook her head at the same time to confirm her words. "The way I remember it, he said you were the kind of fellow that looked better in the dark." Red dotted both cheeks when she let that out.

Ma stopped kneading dough long enough to reply, "Lucky delights in turning a yarn just to see who will believe it." Cowboy nodded. "Why just before he went back to the blacksmith forge," she continued, "your big scamp of a husband asked me if I planned to make a batch of biscuits for each year my eldest here was prodigal." All three laughed.

Cowboy said lightly, "Appears Lucky might jes' care more for a stock of good biscuits than to actual seeing me again."

The big door at the front of the house opened without warning. An older man, slightly stooped, stepped in. The long black coat, his vest and trousers, together with the round-topped preacher's hat bore dust from his ride on the Atascosa roads. He stopped long enough to survey the scene around the table. The parson took in a deep sniff of the cooking aromas before focusing on the clump of dough in his wife's hands. Then he eyeballed the stranger. Cowboy stood to greet him.

The man approached, saying, "Biscuits in the making when Ma's birthday comes day after tomorrow. New horse in the paddock, and Lucky out in the barn grinning like a jackass eating briars." He stopped in front of Cowboy, almost height enough to look him eye-to-eye. "Can only mean one thing," he said, his usual sonorous voice no longer steady, "You've come home to us."

His words, "Praise God!" and Cowboy's murmured, "Pa," got muffled somewhere in each other's neck as the two bear-hugged in a telling grip. Both women let flow tears of joy where they stood; to them the sight too precious. Stepping back finally from the embrace, Pa took an appraising look at his son. He grabbed the offered hand to pump over and over again. "First tell us you'll stay, then assure us you paid real money for that big buckskin outside. After that you can speak of your journey."

Cowboy could only nod, his voice lost for now. He knew it would take minutes, and a bit more of Ma's hot coffee to recover.

Pa sat opposite him at the table. He tossed his hat in a nearby chair. From a back pocket he took a kerchief to rub his nose before accepting the steaming cup Ma handed him. Seeing the sheer exhaustion in the parson's face, she asked, "How was the all-night vigil at Widow Jenkin's house?"

The man raised his eyes from the cup. "Martha's fever broke much, much sooner than the Doc expected. Said he'd never seen anything like it. Expects her to live." He spooned sugar into the coffee, tasted it, and smiled his approval. "I thought that most providentially strange, until I saw you." Pa nodded to Cowboy. "I know now that God meant me to hurry home." He placed his big hand on that of Cowboy's. "Two miracles in the space of one morning. I am doubly blessed."

***

Cowboy could not imagine doing this belabored task on any August afternoon. Rhythmic creaking of the thick wooden handle, the accompanying burst of hissing air, followed apace by its loud intake again created the only sound within the open barn. The big man tugged a blacksmith's bellows without stopping. Broken ember chunks, the remains of fired mesquite glowed intense orangey-red. An almost invisible flame flickered along their top. The small forge's heat reddened the wrangler's face. His chest bare beneath the leather apron, his back and neck all dripped sweat.

"You've got to make it hotter this time," Lucky shouted, "or the weld will just break again." The smaller man struggled to hold the two jagged pieces of broken lift rod in the fire at the proper angle. Balancing one on each shoulder, he held the tips of both centered in the brightest glow.

Cowboy redoubled his effort, pumping faster, and watching the color slowly become almost white. After a quarter hour, the rod tips radiated a similar hue.

"Now," Lucky yelled. He passed off one rod to his brother as they both hurried to the anvil horn where the two ends, already disturbed and beaten into scarfing angles, met to form one continuous metal shaft. Lucky struck at this new seam over and again. He rotated the metal, banging away again until the lift rod lost its heat.

Cowboy watched his brother's eyes to gauge the other's satisfaction with the work. First a slight nod, then another. Lucky grinned but did not address the metal at their knees. "I'll wager you rather be in this barn mastering smithy chores, than sitting around the kitchen playing mama's boy to a woman that won't seem to let you out of her sight again."

The big man looked over one shoulder before nodding his agreement.

"Best we let this weld cool of its own," Lucky said. "No water this time. I'll take the hammer to it in the morning, strike the seam and see if she'll hold this time." He shook his head, experiencing some doubt.

Cowboy struggled to unknot the tangled apron strings behind his back. His eye caught sight of the makeshift contrivance in the corner. What at one time must have been a buggy's wheel, now went without the steel rim and the curved wooden felloes. Every extended spoke now sported thin, hand-hewn oaken staves; each affixed to the wheel hub by a stout rivet. Cowboy speculated that the metal rod protruding where the axel arm should be meant this to be a clumsy attempt at a windmill wheel. He looked at Lucky, now putting away the tongs and hammer. But the wrangler said nothing.

Both men grabbed up belongings, walked the short way to the well's pump, and doused themselves clean with buckets of clear water.

As they dried and donned shirts and hats once more, a clatter could be heard from inside the kitchen nearby. "Uh-oh, big brother," Lucky said with a laugh. "Best we *vamonos toda prisa* before the women put us to doing jobs we're no good at." He snapped a suspender over one shoulder, all but running to saddle the bay. "Got to go check the sluice on the back property line,' he said as he mounted up. "River in the north county up on its banks already. Francisco Perez and San Miguel Creeks show they're beginning to rise." He nodded. "Must be raining something fierce way up in the Hill Country."

Cowboy shot him a query with raised eyebrows, to which the younger brother replied, "Come to think on it, you don't know about the sluice." He shrugged, searching his mind for when this was built. "We fill this big stock pond each year with runoff from spring rains. Mostly it's enough water to last when the creek winds down to a trickle. Let's us raise other than longhorn cattle, which don't seem to need regular water."

Cowboy rode his big horse in silence, as he usually did on the trail. He felt no need at that moment to speak about cattle, family, or travels to Lucky. He calculated it a slim chance to get a word in while his brother rambled on about the construction detail of the narrow channel run between the creek and the pond.

The wrangler judged that Lucky sold a story short for once. Setting his eye upon the hand-dug gully carrying water to a meandering reservoir, Cowboy knew this had been a massive undertaking. He said, "I can remember there being a shallow *barranco* right about here. That ravine wadn't no more than hip deep."

"That's right," Lucky said. "And fifty yards wide. Used to open out into those mesquite breaks yonder." He pointed southeast to open land. So's we took what's dug up making the sluice and dammed the far end." His unexpected laugh caught Cowboy unawares. "That bank did not hold the first year, and we lost most of the water. Now it works just fine."

Cowboy dismounted the buckskin to take a closer look at the water moving across the spillway. It moved at a slow but steady stream through the sluice before rippling down the bank. The collected pool already covered the tank's bottom all the distance to the far embankment. The wrangler judged it would fill in about a week's time.

His attention shifted when he felt Dusty jerk at the reins Cowboy held in his hand. He focused on the rider approaching through the brush. From the pony's relaxed gait, it appeared to be a friendly visit by someone no stranger to the ranch. "Who might that be?" Cowboy asked. "He sets a saddle well," nodding his approval, "For sure knows how to ride a horse."

That drew a grin from Lucky, but no words. He waited further exposition, but got none. His brother seemed too engaged in watching the rider's effortless skill. "Oh, that would be Lee McAllister," he said. "Inherited the old Potter Ranch next door when the aunt and uncle died childless."

The rider topped the slight rise, reined in the chestnut pony, and glanced at both men with no particular hurry. "Afternoon, pard," Lee said to Lucky in firm tones, but turned to look straight at Cowboy. From underneath the rider's dark felt hat, green eyes narrowed. Hair the color of just-cut hay jutted from the brim long enough to cover both ears and a bit of cheek. Cowboy judged it likely grew past the rear neckband of the wrinkled wool shirt. A red wind rag wrapped twice around the neck. Its fancy knot secured the bandana in place, one long end loosely draped over the right shoulder while the other hung down to cover the top button of the open collar.

"Who's your friend there?" Lee asked. Green eyes moved up and down, assessing the big man before any identity given.

Lucky flashed an impish grin. "Oh, that's my eldest brother," he said. The one I been telling you about; gone missing all this time."

Cowboy stared back in return. Something about this trim cowpoke with chaps hanging down to boot heels, and an almost new lariat tied to the saddle did not square in his mind. Not until the head turned and he could see full profile.

"You the one went off to see the elephant?" Lee asked Cowboy directly. The voice came softer this time, still full of interest.

"Yes, ma'am," the wrangler answered. He realized the rider now holding his gaze to be a woman

"So, how was it?" she asked, crossed forearms over her saddle horn, and waited the telling of his tale.

***

As ranch rides go, Cowboy counted the amble home from the stock pond enjoyable: a mild afternoon with the promise of warming, the company of two good riders on two good horses, and the sheer joy Dusty seemed to show knowing this range might be a place to settle. They loped three abreast through the scrub and mesquite thickets. Lee rode between and slightly in front of the two brothers; turning her head as she conversed with Lucky, turning back as she just watched Cowboy ride.

He said little more than "yes" or "no" when addressed with questions, concentrating more on the talk between Lucky and the young woman. By the time this trio reached the homestead, the wrangler learned that Lee had owned and worked the Potter Ranch for no more than a year, mostly by herself. Her uncle's two ranch hands left soon after the funeral, themselves too old to be much help any longer. Lucky helped out in their stead as best he could. This undaunted woman who sat a horse with such ease also took spiritual counsel from the two men's father, and even from their brother, Marcus, whenever that young parson came to Atascosa. Cowboy smiled almost without showing it. Lee McAllister was a hard working, God-fearing woman. She also had need of an experienced ranch hand.

Two buggies sat beside the house as they approached. One jacketed completely in dust, the other newer with an almost pristine appearance. The carriage horses rested without motion, except for the occasional fly swat.

"Now *everyone* is here," Lucky said. His good cheer sounded as genuine as it did heartfelt. He slid off the bay and tied leathers, not waiting for his companions. He hurried through the front door. From within, merry voices talking one over the other, plus the constant yelp of children's laughter could be heard.

Cowboy let Lee precede him into the room. At his entry, all conversation stopped. Even the three young children held their noise to stare up at the tall stranger. A single man rose. Slightly shorter than Lucky, but eighteen months his senior, Marcus walked without hesitation to his older brother. He threw his arms around him in a tight clench, but said not a word. "I thought about you many times on the trail, *hermano*," Cowboy said at last.

In return, the spirited preacher from Uvalde replied, "In my daily prayers, I asked for this moment to come." He showed the small beginnings of a smile. "Now all of us are blessed." They hugged again with even greater warmth. Ma and Caroline cried quietly into their aprons.

Stepping back from that warm embrace, Cowboy looked into the eyes of a near stranger, the kid brother they affectionately all called "little Johnny". The man standing before the wrangler, no longer a tow-headed urchin of twelve, stood almost to Cowboy's own height. Johnny's strapping torso gave him the clear weight advantage over the older brother. He grabbed Cowboy's extended hand with such a crushing grip that the eldest brother immediately wondered what Ma had been feeding the boy all this time.

Johnny said to him, "You probably don't remember me much on account I was so young when you left. But do know that I was the one that missed you the most." His longing look searched Cowboy's face. "I always looked up to you. You did everything better, stronger, and smarter than the rest of us."

Johnny shifted from one big foot to the other until Cowboy pulled him, too, into an embrace. It crossed the wrangler's mind what misjudgment this hug might be when his wind got near choked out of him by a squeeze worthy of the monster bear that day at the cave.

"Let him go, you big galoot. It's my turn." The man got elbowed aside by a most pregnant mother-to-be. Cowboy did not recall the little lady's voice all at once, but he did know the eyes on top of that smile. She'd flashed them at him often enough as an irrepressible little tomboy: Alice, Riley Culpepper's little sister. She stepped in to clinch arms around his waist for a brief but warm hug. "Truth is," she said, "none of us thought we'd see you alive again. Word actually came of your unfortunate demise."

At that, Cowboy laughed. He turned to look at the only unfamiliar person in the room. This woman sat at the kitchen table next to his Ma. With her free arm, she clutched a pair of lookalike young boys. In her lap their little sister cuddled. Marcus did the honors, 'This is my wife, Lydia, the twins, Gideon and Nathanael, and our daughter, Hannah."

The woman smiled the warm greeting of a dedicated preacher's wife. "We've brought a cake for your mother's birthday, but she insists that we dedicate it instead to celebrate your return." Lydia patted Ma's forearm before nodding to a spot across the room. "Also, Alice has made some of her wonderful punch." She smiled again as though she'd known Cowboy all her life. "We'll have that after supper. I'm glad you could join us here today."

Cowboy said his thanks and greeting. He took her hand briefly, but his curiosity about Lee's role in all of this stole most of his attention. That query got somewhat addressed when his Ma stepped over to the only female at this gathering fitted out in riding duds. She took the young woman by the elbow to lead her nearly face-to-face with her eldest son. "I see that you've already met our Leanora here," his mother said to him.

"Yes," Cowboy responded in a soft baritone. "It's a lovely name."

Two circles of red grew on very tanned cheeks. The new owner of Potter's Ranch wished to be anywhere else in the world that moment; just not in this suddenly crowded room. Redness deepened when she heard Cowboy choke back his laughter. Yet, she relaxed a bit when she saw the seeds of gentleness begin to flicker in his eyes.

***

"If I can reach it with the palm of my hand, then it's too short to be a windmill." Johnny proved his point to Lucky by setting his empty punch glass atop the wooden cross piece without even needing to stand on tiptoes. Marcus and Pa nodded as Lucky muttered incoherence and kicked dirt with his boot. "You should have made it taller," the youngest brother went on. "But so far it hasn't blown over yet. And I believe you told Ma it's pumped maybe ten gallons in the six months since you planted it." At that remark a round of belly laughs burst out from everyone—everyone except Cowboy.

"It just needs more help is all," the wrangler said evenly.

"Then let us pray he gets it soon," Marcus said with mirth. "Or else he'll spend even more time trying to piece together that hand-me-down metal into a working machine."

Lucky startled the others when he jerked himself around to square off with them, leaning shoulders forward, fists raised chest-high. Cowboy judged that dark look on his face meant Lucky had determined to brawl. The younger brother stared each of the siblings in the eye. Studiously, he avoided Pa's stern look.

Lucky spit out, "Go ahead, it's easy for you to laugh. I'm the one bounden to work this hardscrabble ranch." His body shook with pent up feelings. "Just me, Caroline, and Ma. Pa when he don't have no parson chores. I'm not the one what caught the eye of the banker's daughter and got me a job in town. And I didn't get the Gospel call as a boy and take up Devil chasing in Uvalde." Then he turned to Cowboy standing closest to him. "We're getting by, but just barely. Nothing left over to get us anything like a real windmill." He breathed in labored gasps before his voice trailed off with, "These days it's hard to sell cattle to just about anyone." The glare from his focused stare all but carried heat to Cowboy's face.

"We'll have no more of that talk," Pa began to admonish his next-to-youngest.

Cowboy waived his father off with a big hand. He stepped up close to his querulous brother. To him he said, "Is this about the windmill, or is something on your mind you mean to say to me direct?"

Lucky raised himself up, trying to stretch to the same height as Cowboy. When he realized that would never happen, he let out a sigh and took a half-step back. "You leaving in such a hurry," he said, "left us all flat-footed. And, you've been gone so long." Hands spread in front of his chest, wide enough to pass his shoulders. "Now you're back again. It caught us all flat-footed once more." He looked around for affirmation, but found none. "Well, me anyway," he said. Arms fell to his sides as his anger sank into dismay. In a plaintive voice now tinged with hurt, Lucky said, "It ain't right you just showing up out of nowhere and expecting to take over the ranch just 'cause you're the oldest."

For a second, no sound could be heard except for the women conversing on the porch. Yet at that instant Cowboy's face lit up with gut-felt relief. He grinned. His new comfort came from the realization that he had now completed the circle of his journey. It began with a fistfight and now might finish with another. Of ending that way, he saw no need. The wrangler asked, "That what got you vexed up like a young bull at the first sign of spring? Me pulling this place out from under you? Until I spoke with Riley Culpepper last week in Schulenburg, I didn't know there even was a ranch to come home to." He laughed at his own misconception.

"What?!" came almost simultaneously from all three younger brothers. Pa just nodded at this curiosity, as if he had seen it coming all along.

Cowboy ignored their question to say, "I already told Ma and Pa here, I ain't going nowhere as long as I can spend what time we got left being with them. You worked the ranch all this while, it's yours to run." He nodded to himself first, then to Lucky. "I will help out best I can where's it you need me, but only as *segundo* to you." Cowboy's big grin returned. He stepped up to Lucky with a big hand extended. "Unless you go off and do somethin' plum locoed, like try and steal a biscuit off my breakfast plate." Cowboy turned to the others with a wink. "A kid brother will do that to a fella."

This time Lucky lead the laughter as he pumped the hand offered. His eyes took on a guarded look of merriment. "And this?" he nodded, indicating the gallows-like wooden structure.

"Oh, I think I might could help you a bit more with that," Cowboy said.

Pa indicated for his sons to gather close. They did so without hesitation, evidencing years of practice. "The parable of the prodigal son," he said, "in the Book of Luke has no ending. Jesus just stopped talking where He did. To this day it is unclear what exactly the older brother did in the days that followed." The preacher put one hand on Lucky. "In our case, a younger brother worked the fields while the older brother went away." He then set the other hand on Cowboy. "This brother here certainly did not take family riches with him to squander in far off places. From what I can tell, his was a journey of the spirit. Now he has returned. No fatted calf. Merely a birthday cake shared with his mother." The preacher stood back, indicating all of them with a sweeping hand. "As in the parable, each of you has got to decide, 'how will I act now toward my returning brother?'" He paused, before adding, "Both today and in the days to come." They answered his challenge by slapping Cowboy playfully, but somewhat roughly on the back and shoulders.

Marcus and Johnny soon joined their Pa on the walk back to the house. Without speaking, they knew enough to leave Lucky with Cowboy by themselves to work out any remaining misgivings.

To Cowboy's questioning look, Lucky responded, "I didn't mean to have such a case of the grouch just now." For a moment he studied his boot leathers. "It's a kick in the gut when you work calluses on your fingers month-in-and-month-out, got no money for any trivials, and your best efforts to build something needed draw only scorn." Still looking down he reached to pull something from a back pocket. "When I read this and then got poked fun at I saw everything slipping away. Truth is, I was happy as all get out when you first rode up. Even liked working together in the barn. But as I thought on it more, I got scared." Lucky looked up. "For a moment, it seemed like you came home to rescue your little brother just like you always did. The white knight once more." He handed the telegram to Cowboy. Lucky said, "The look in your eyes just now tells me I got it all wrong. I apologize. You mean this as a gift to all of us with only sincerity in your heart."

Cowboy read aloud, "Flint & Walling Model 12 Star windmill freighted to you by San Antonio Machine & Supply Company. Expect next ten days. Gift from the returning wanderer. Regards, Riley Culpepper, Esq."

Looking up from the page, Cowboy said, "It's a long tale for another time. Short ways, I'll just say it's honest bought. All that time on the trail with not much to spend wages on if you don't give in to temptations of the flesh."

Lucky looked up to the pale blue eyes of his older brother. "I don't give a good fried apple where the money came from," he said. His face mellowed into a soft smile. "I'll just say thanks and be grateful."

Cowboy threw one arm around Lucky's neck. They walked to join the others on the porch.

***

In a mood of idleness after the breakfast meal, Cowboy watched the bent pewter spoon continuously push coffee into a swirl as he stirred it round the cup and around again. The porcelain clutched in one palm felt almost hot to the touch; comforting on this cool morning. Steam wet his face and eyebrows as he sat bent over the table taking in fresh aroma. His own dented container that he drank from daily on the trail lay still hidden in the leathers of his saddlebag now pegged up in the barn. Home life, he thought to himself, with all it promised of hard work, would be a pure pleasure getting used to.

Pa set the brass cartridge back onto the table's top with a clang. That noise broke the spell of Cowboy's silent reverie. Pa said, "You say that's a .50 caliber rifle?" The Big Fifty leaned against an empty chair. Cowboy nodded, taking pleasure from his father's obvious delight in the examination of the Sharps buffalo gun; a gift of the prodigal's journey from his oldest son. With some amazement, the parson picked up the bullet once more to place it across his palm as if to demonstrate. From tip of the rounded lead to the base of the flattened rim, the cartridge stretched the entire width of the man's broad hand. With a jesting grin, but mock-serious tones, Pa announced, "Jackalopes of south Texas beware. Now I have fierce new armament, and shall fear thee no longer. Best you hide when you see me approach." He looked at Cowboy across the table with dead-set eyes.

"They squirrel away now already, don't they?" Cowboy asked.

"True," Pa said. "But now I shall know the reason why."

They both laughed at his jest.

Ma laughed, too, as she stepped up with the offer of more hot coffee from the stove. She said nothing. As her son's eyes met hers, she merely touched the brooch pinned to her blouse with extended fingertips. Her smile made the entirety of his heart begin to feel warm as the coffee in his grip. "It looks good on you, Ma," he said, after choking back a small lump forming at the front of his throat.

"Tell me that story again," she requested, set the big pot on the table, and seated herself to listen.

Cowboy was quick to indulge her. A carved alabaster likeness of an unknown but undoubtedly beautiful woman held fast to the translucent seashell back piece. This cameo jewelry Ma now wore evidenced superb and patient craftsmanship. He said, "The last time I chanced to visit my old saddle pal Ray and his pretty wife Esmeralda in Cowtown, she pressed me to buy you a grand keepsake from my travels to give you when I finally reached Atascosa again." He thought of that afternoon with sweet recall. "I guess it's always easy for a person to spend someone else's money, but I didn't mind." He looked at the brooch once more. "She took me to this fancy store on the good side of town. Folks there knew her, so the trade seemed fair." Cowboy tapped a place on the side of his chest beneath the arm where his coat would have touched. "Didn't dwell on it at the time, but seems I always carried it in the pocket here, next to my heart." Her smile swelled from mere fondness to that of a mother's unbounded love.

Captured still by her affection she asked, "You are going to help out Leanora today, are you not?"

"Yes, ma'am," Cowboy said. "Lucky is sending me there in his place. Reckon he'll be doing that steady once the windmill parts arrive."

"She's a fine woman, don't you think?" Ma asked. She did not even begin to hide the twinkle now in her eye. Pa looked on as if this were to be expected, and something in which he certainly should not meddle.

"Yes, ma'am," her son said again. "I know she can ride. Today I'll see how she sets with cattle." His twinkle began to match her own.

***

How she set with cattle, Cowboy could not easily determine at this distance. He seemed of two minds, sitting on Dusty some quarter-mile back-trailed, watching. On one hand, Lee worked the stock with an uneasy resolve. Not nearly as effortless as Lucky, she herded the beeves with a nonetheless resolute determination. On the other hand, he could tell that more days dogging the Herefords on this ranch would have her as his brother's equal.

Two pair of young white-face split off from the milling beeves, catching Lee on the far side. To chase them meant giving up control of the herd she now pushed single-handed toward the watering tank. Her eyes betrayed evil thoughts toward these four delinquents, but her concentration remained with the other cattle. Lee did not see Cowboy until he cantered Dusty to cut the strays off from the open land they now trotted towards. Their leader dashed at a quick right angle to the horse and rider as those two approached the strays head-on. Dusty lunged in front of the yearling, cutting off his advance. The Hereford wheeled an opposite direction to race past the horse that way. Again the buckskin cut off his advance. Cowboy did little more than touch Dusty's sides with one knee or the other, to let the big horse know which way to anticipate.

After a minute-and-a-half of such twists and false turns, the Hereford stopped, looked at the horse and rider blocking his path, and gave up the effort by turning back the way he had come with his followers in tow. Five more minutes and the four were back with the herd.

"Morning," Cowboy said with all due pleasantry. A greeting Lee returned in kind.

She wondered aloud, "Do all the brothers handle cattle as well as you and Lucky?"

"Been known to," he said with a grin, "Not likely so much anymore. Marcus and Johnny got else on their minds."

"And you're better at it than the other three, I'd say," Lee said, watching for his reaction.

Cowboy replied nothing to that, or to the appraising look she covered him with for a long moment. "If you're looking for a top hand to help you mind your ranch," he said, "I'd be obliged if you'd give me some consideration. Lucky could use me some, but really not all that much. He has a good handle on it."

Lee liked his direct but understated approach. "What did you have in mind?" she asked.

"I figure it's easier on all of us to run your stock and ours as one big herd. We got no fences and share the water now as it is," he said. "Got this new pal up north of Cowtown name of Calvin Quinn; married to a good Christian woman. She's gone and adopted me like some big brother or uncle." Cowboy shifted in the saddle to face Lee more directly. "They run a feedlot together that sells beef back east. Cal says he'll buy all the good cattle I'll bring him." He watched Lee take all this in with calm consideration.

After a moment's thought, Lee said, "Sure. I figure that's worth a try." She smiled at this man she'd taken an instant liking to. "I'll take you on. We'll work out the particulars with Lucky, but I can see this turning into something good." After a moment more she added, "You have a lot more cattle experience than me. I'll watch and learn."

"Yes ma'am," Cowboy said the third time that morning. "But you're the boss."

Lee laughed at the irony of that. She followed Cowboy and Dusty as he began to push the cattle to water. "One thing I'd like to ask, if it's not too personal," she said. "Lucky claims they called the four of you the Gospel Brothers. He never explained the reason." Lee hesitated. "Would you mind telling me why?"

Cowboy grinned at that old nickname. "I saw you flinch when Ma called you Leonora. You prefer to go by Lee. We have that in common." He drew Dusty up next to her mount. "Folks call me Eden, but even that's not the exact name. I was born Mathew Edenfield DeWitt."

Lee looked at him not fully understanding this as an answer to her question.

He continued, "Pa is a powerful man of God. He names us boys Mathew, Mark, Luke, and John. Me, Marcus, Lucky, and little Johnny—the Gospel Brothers. Any wonder we changed our names?"

211

Lee let this sink in a bit. Then she smiled with a budding new affection. She spurred her horse, calling over a shoulder, "Come on. We got cattle to chase, Eden."

He bobbed a head in agreement, stirring his own mount.

Turning their horses toward the now moving herd, they loped the trail at an easy pace.

Their journey together had *just* begun.

Nonesuch
Study Questions

1. As Pa said, each person in the family had a choice of how he would act toward his brothers, like in the parable of the prodigal son. Do you have more trouble showing love toward people like Cowboy or people like Lucky? How does knowing Jesus loves you allow you to show love to others?

2. Cowboy brought gifts for his family on his return that reminded him of specific stories of God's protection and guidance on his journey. What are some of your memories of God's goodness to you on your journey?

3. Cowboy was concerned about his parents' reaction when he came home, but Ma and Pa accepted him immediately. How is their thrill at Cowboy returning like God's desire for each of us to come back to him? What do you need to do to come home to God?

Epilogue

Epilogue

"I'll go home to my parents, confess what I've done,
And I'll ask them to pardon their prodigal son,
And if they caress me as oft times before,
Then I never will play the Wild Rover no more."

The Wild Rover
Traditional Irish Folksong
Author Unknown

Call to Action

Dear Lord Jesus,

I know that I am a sinner,
and I ask for Your forgiveness.

I believe You died for my sins
and rose from the dead.

I turn from my sins and invite
You to come into my life.

I want to trust and follow
You as my Lord and Savior.

In Your Name.
Amen

Dusty's Song

Dusty's Song

I am an old range rider,
I follow the cattle trail-
Just me and my *caballo,*
Our journey's quite the tale.

I still rope and wrangle,
Can toss a steer with ease,
I spur my big horse Dusty-
To take me where I please.

I've ridden all of Texas,
From the Red to Mexico,
Just runnin' from my sinful past,
To ease my troubled soul.

No matter that I ramble far,
Or miles that Dusty's trod,
I'll find no consolation,
'Til I put my faith in God.

I met our Lord out on the trail,
I looked into His face,
I heard Him call me by my name,
I felt his loving grace.

I'd be quite the liar,
If I was not to tell,
That I believe and I've been saved,
I'm off that road to Hell.

Contact Information

www.facebook.com/DustyAndTheCowboy

DustyAndTheCowboy@gmail.com

www.DustyAndTheCowboy.com